Telling Time

ACTIVITY WORKBOOK

Practice Exercises for
Kindergarten, 1st Grade
and 2nd Grade

Table of Contents

Types of Clocks

There are many different types of clocks!

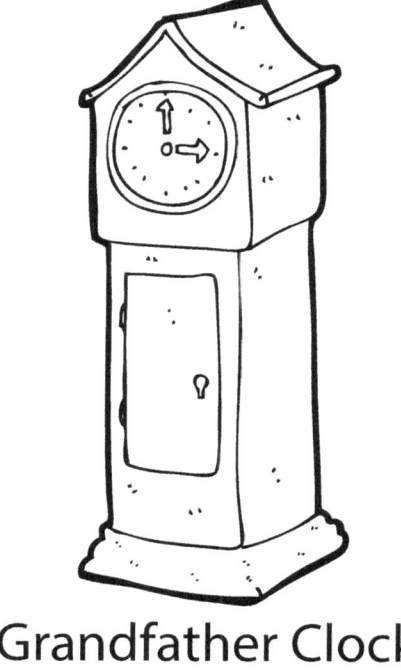

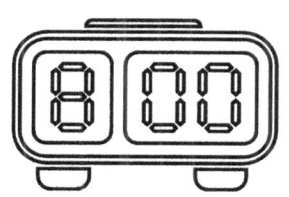

Digital Clock

Analog Clock

Alarm Clock

Grandfather Clock

Draw your favorite clock here:

The Hour Hand

Clocks help us know what time it is!

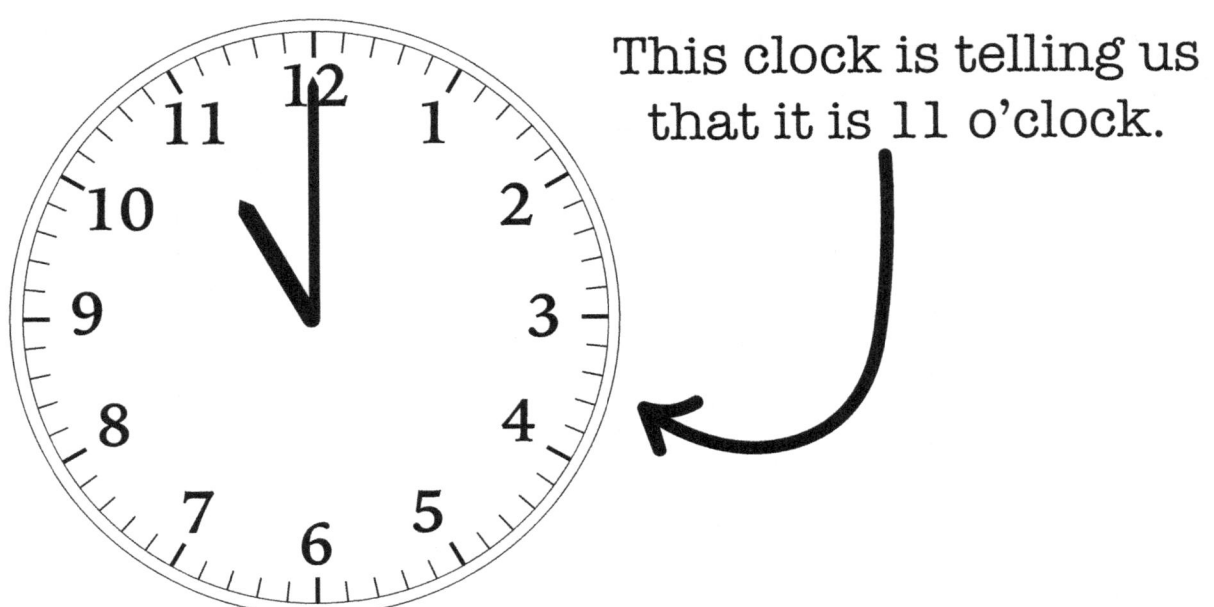

This clock is telling us that it is 11 o'clock.

Practice tracing then writing the word o'clock:

o'clock

o'clock

o'clock

Every clock has twelve numbers. Can you fill in the missing numbers on these clocks?

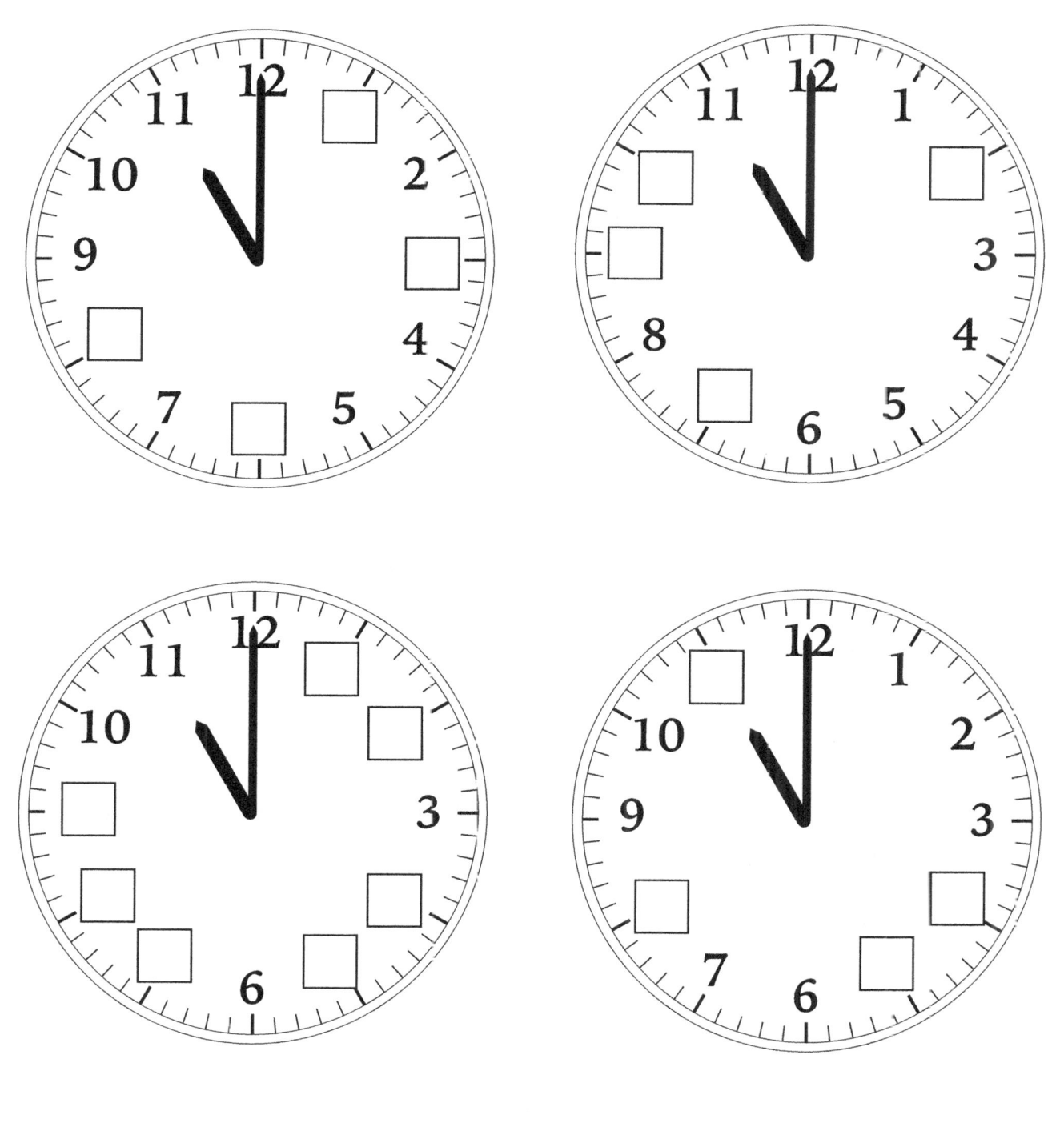

Every clock has two hands. This hand is called the **hour** hand.

The shorter hand tells us what hour it is.

Here, the hour hand points to the 3. That means it is 3 o'clock.

Here, the hour hand points to the 7. That means it is 7 o'clock.

Write in what time it is.

1

7 o'clock

2

☐ o'clock

3

☐ o'clock

4

☐ o'clock

Write in what time it is.

5

☐ o'clock

6

☐ o'clock

7

☐ o'clock

8

☐ o'clock

Write in what time it is.

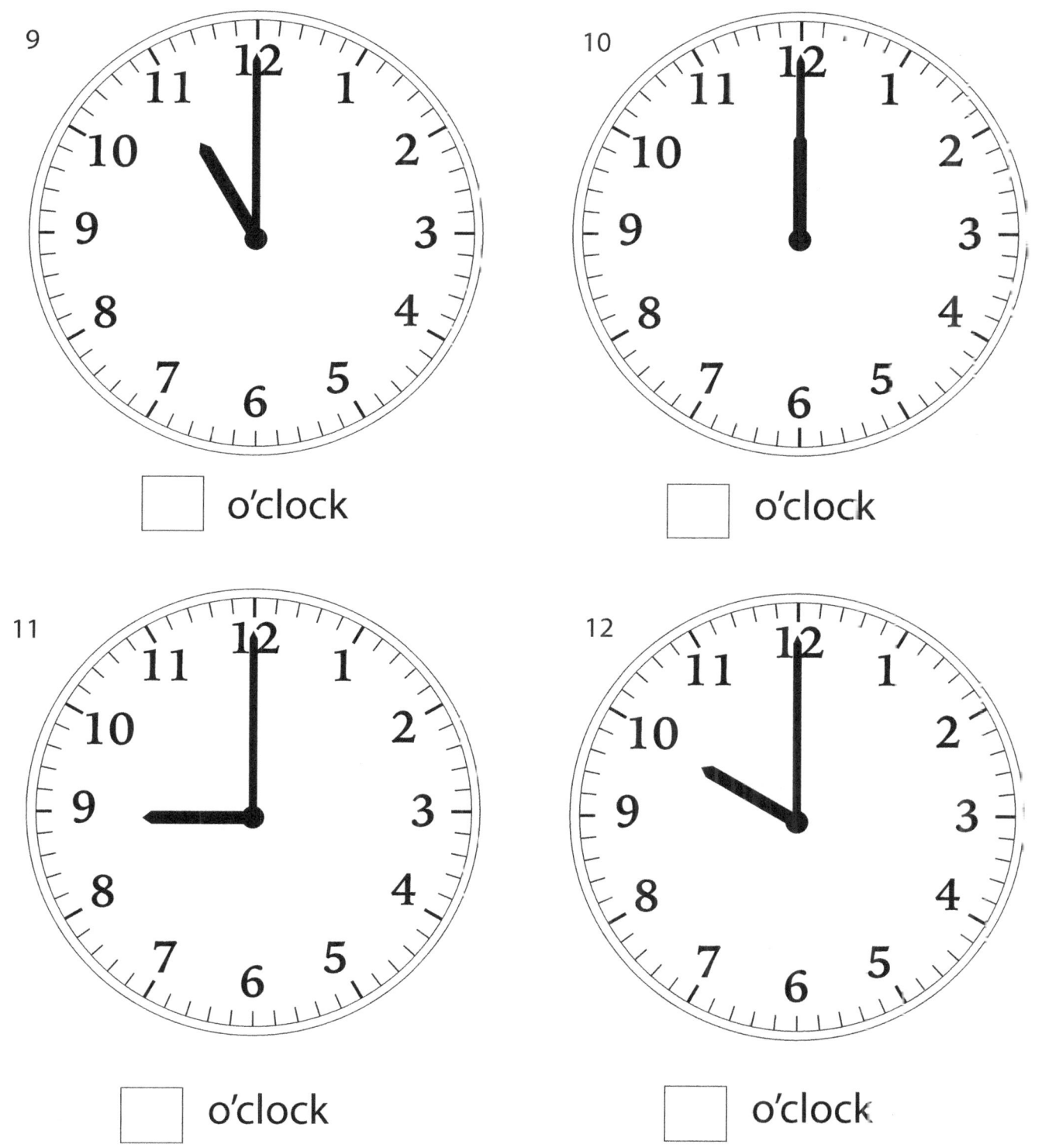

9

[ ] o'clock

10

[ ] o'clock

11

[ ] o'clock

12

[ ] o'clock

Did you know there are different ways to write the time?

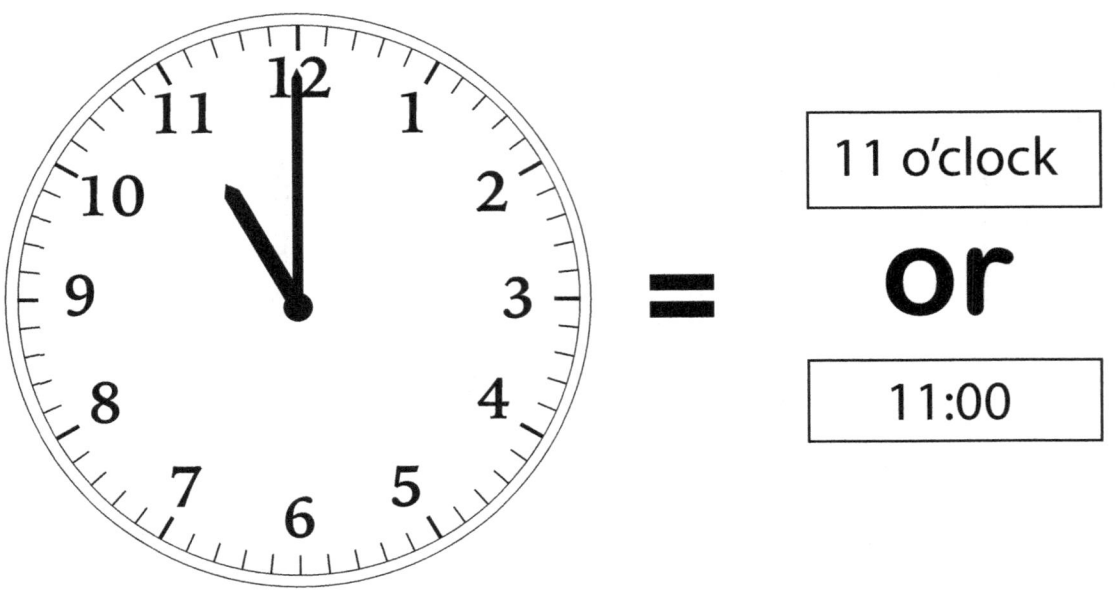

= 11 o'clock

or

11:00

Let's practice writing time this new way!

1   1:00

2   :

8

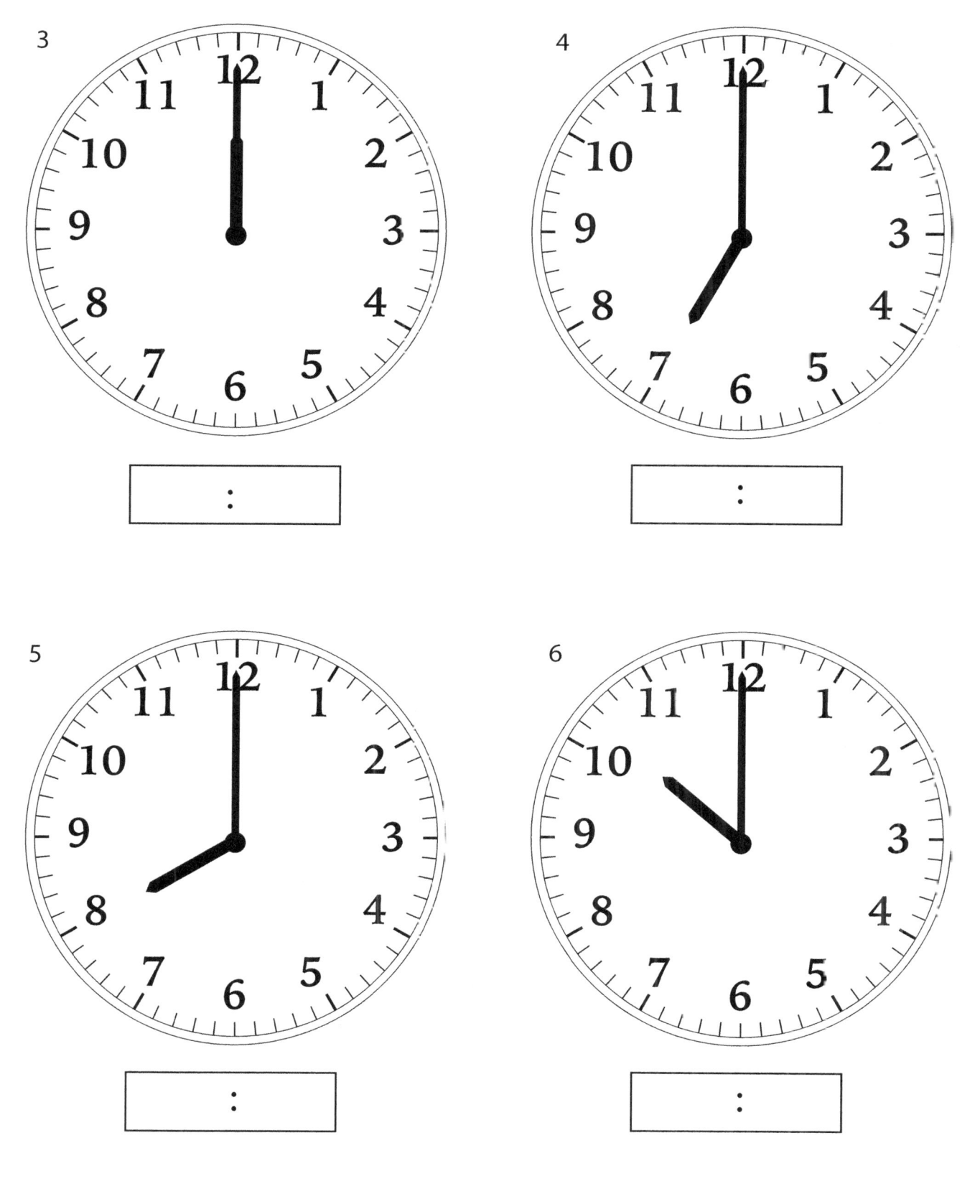

3

:

4

:

5

:

6

:

9

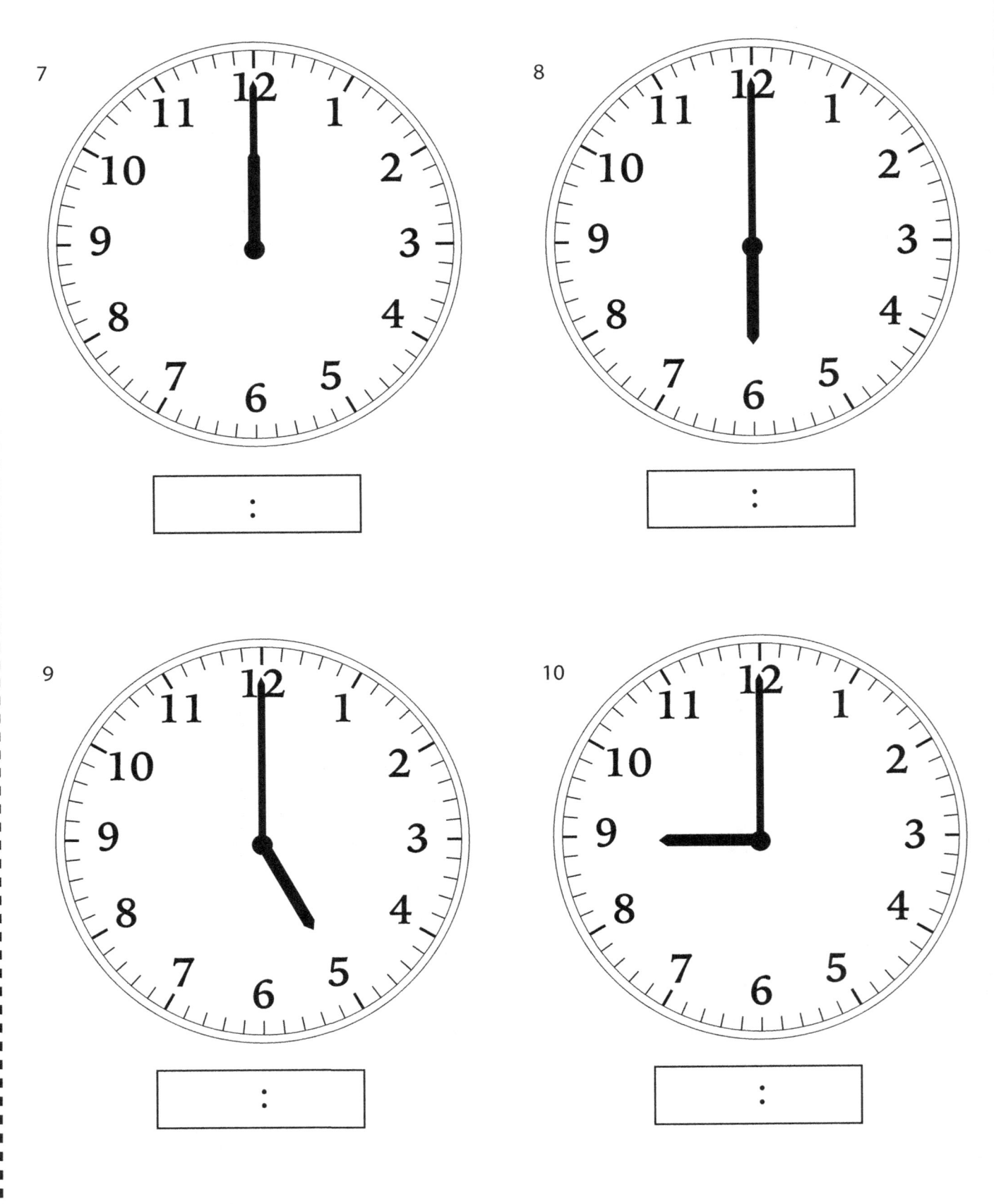

Draw a line connecting the clock to the correct time.

1

2

6:00

8:00

3

11:00

4

7:00

Draw a line connecting the clock to the correct time.

5

| 5:00 |

6

| 3:00 |

7

| 12:00 |

8

| 1:00 |

Draw on the hour hand so that the clock matches the time given.

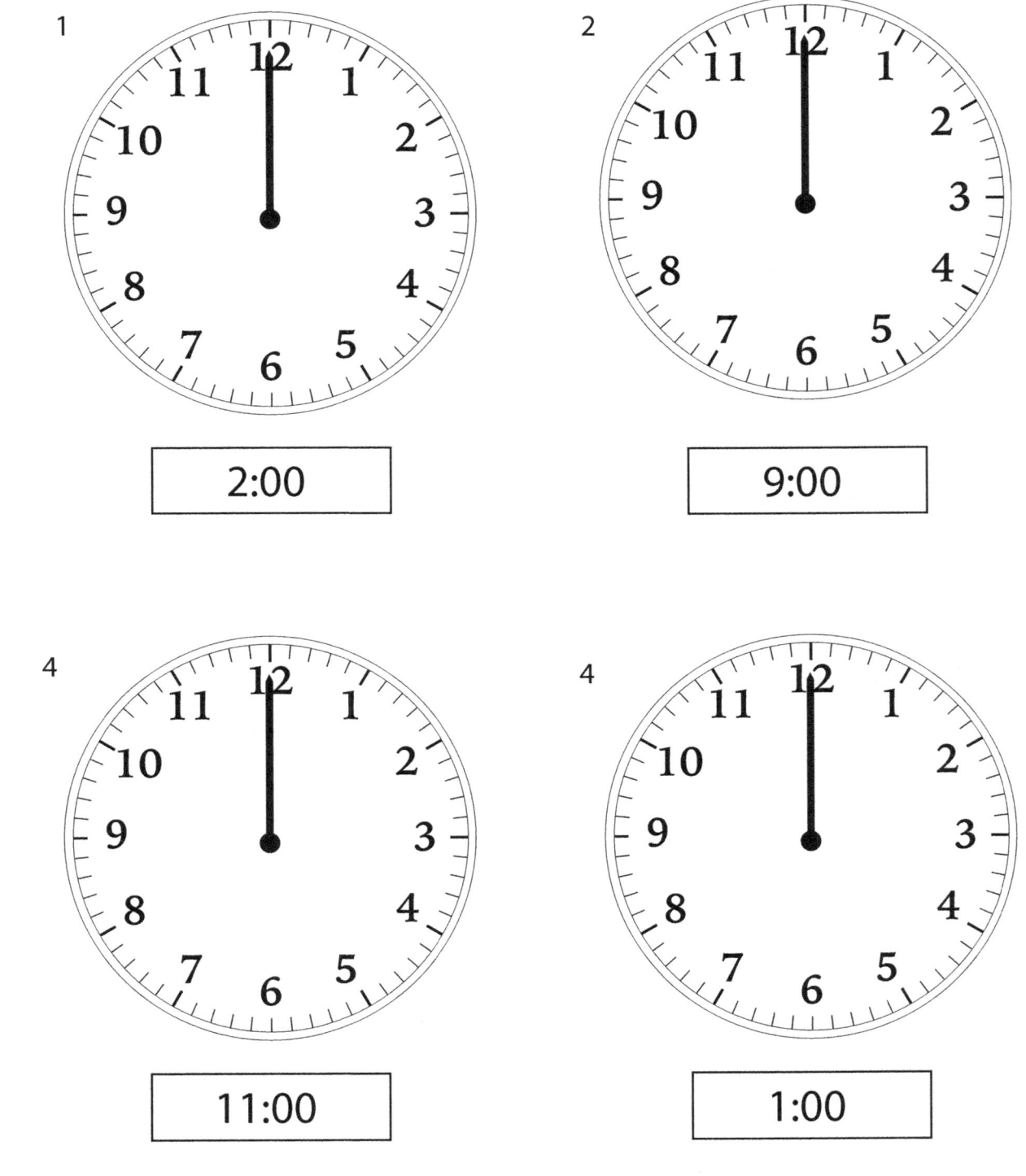

1

2:00

2

9:00

4

11:00

4

1:00

Draw on the hour hand so that the clock matches the time given.

5

3:00

6

12:00

7

8:00

8

4:00

15

Draw on the hour hand so that the clock matches the time given.

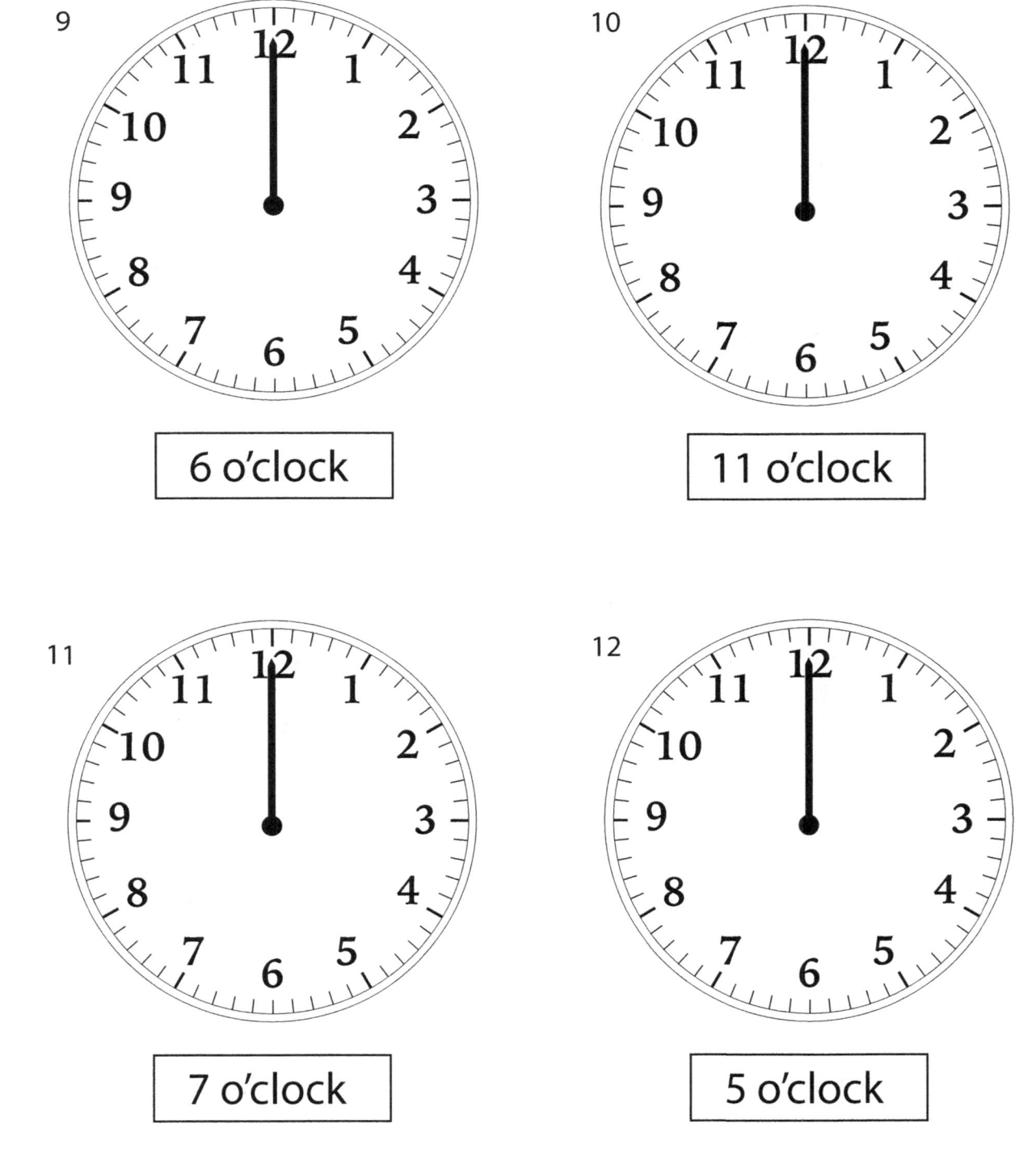

9

6 o'clock

10

11 o'clock

11

7 o'clock

12

5 o'clock

Draw on the hour hand so that the clock matches the time given.

13

8 o'clock

14

9 o'clock

15

10 o'clock

16

2 o'clock

17

Circle the correct time

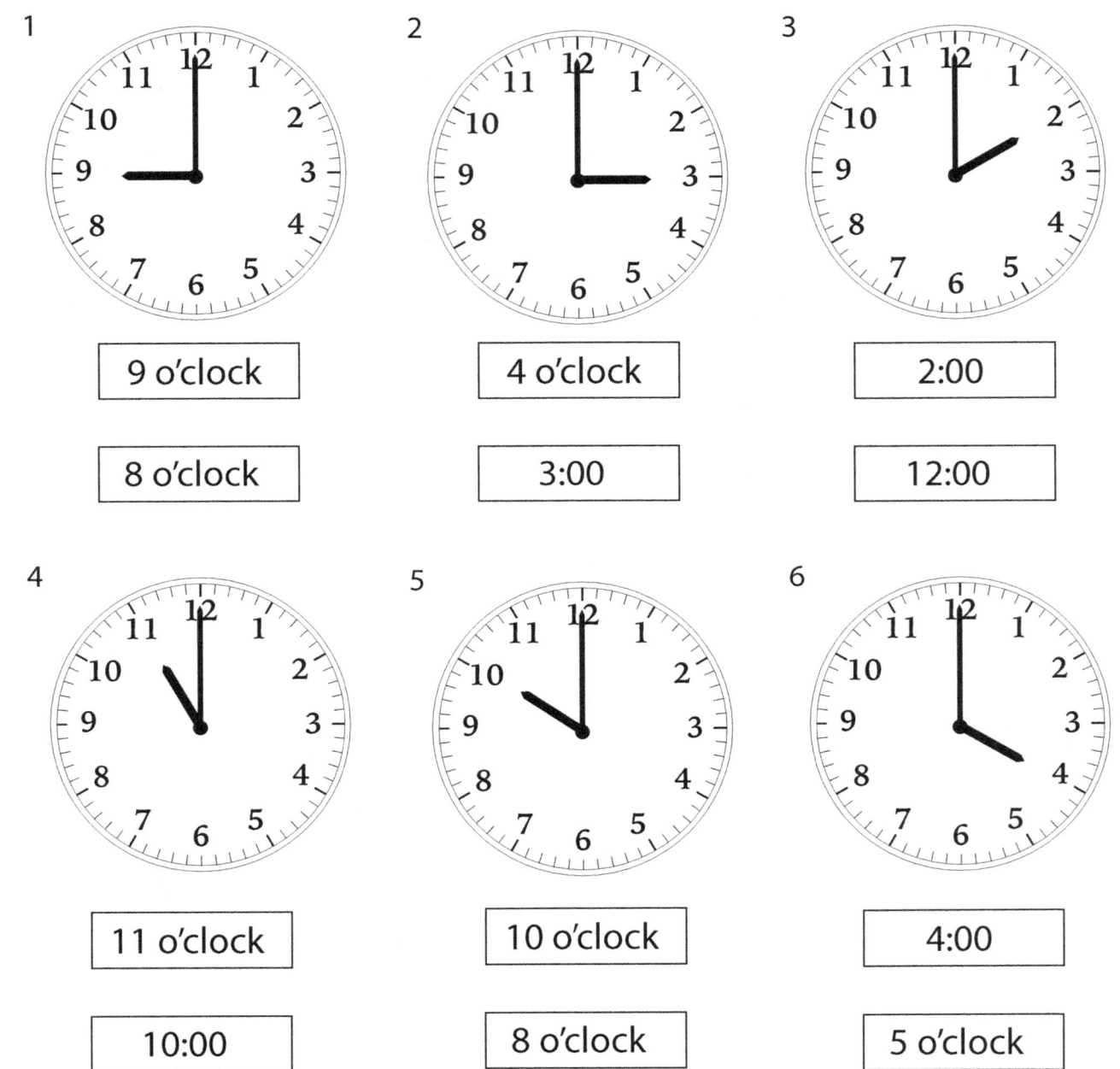

1

9 o'clock

8 o'clock

2

4 o'clock

3:00

3

2:00

12:00

4

11 o'clock

10:00

5

10 o'clock

8 o'clock

6

4:00

5 o'clock

Circle the correct time

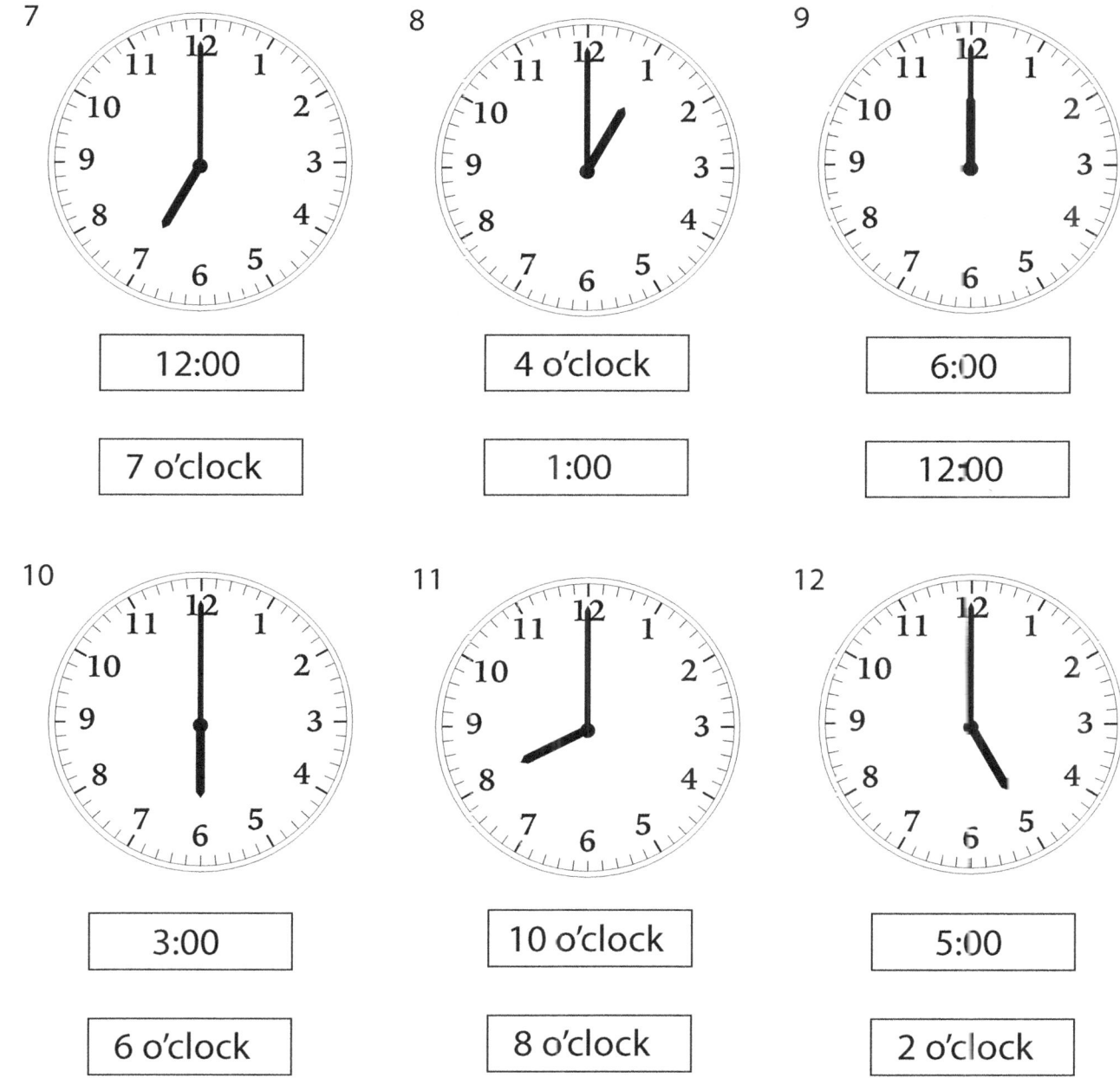

7

12:00

7 o'clock

8

4 o'clock

1:00

9

6:00

12:00

10

3:00

6 o'clock

11

10 o'clock

8 o'clock

12

5:00

2 o'clock

How much time has passed?

Look at the clocks and write in the time. How many hours have passed?

Example:

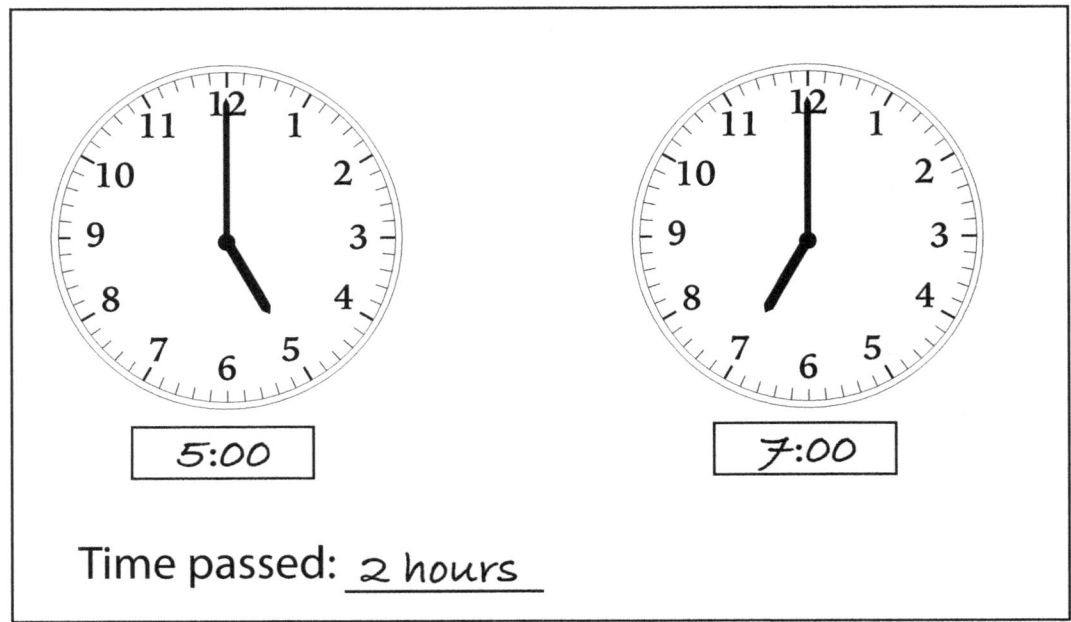

5:00

7:00

Time passed: __2 hours__

1

Time passed: _____

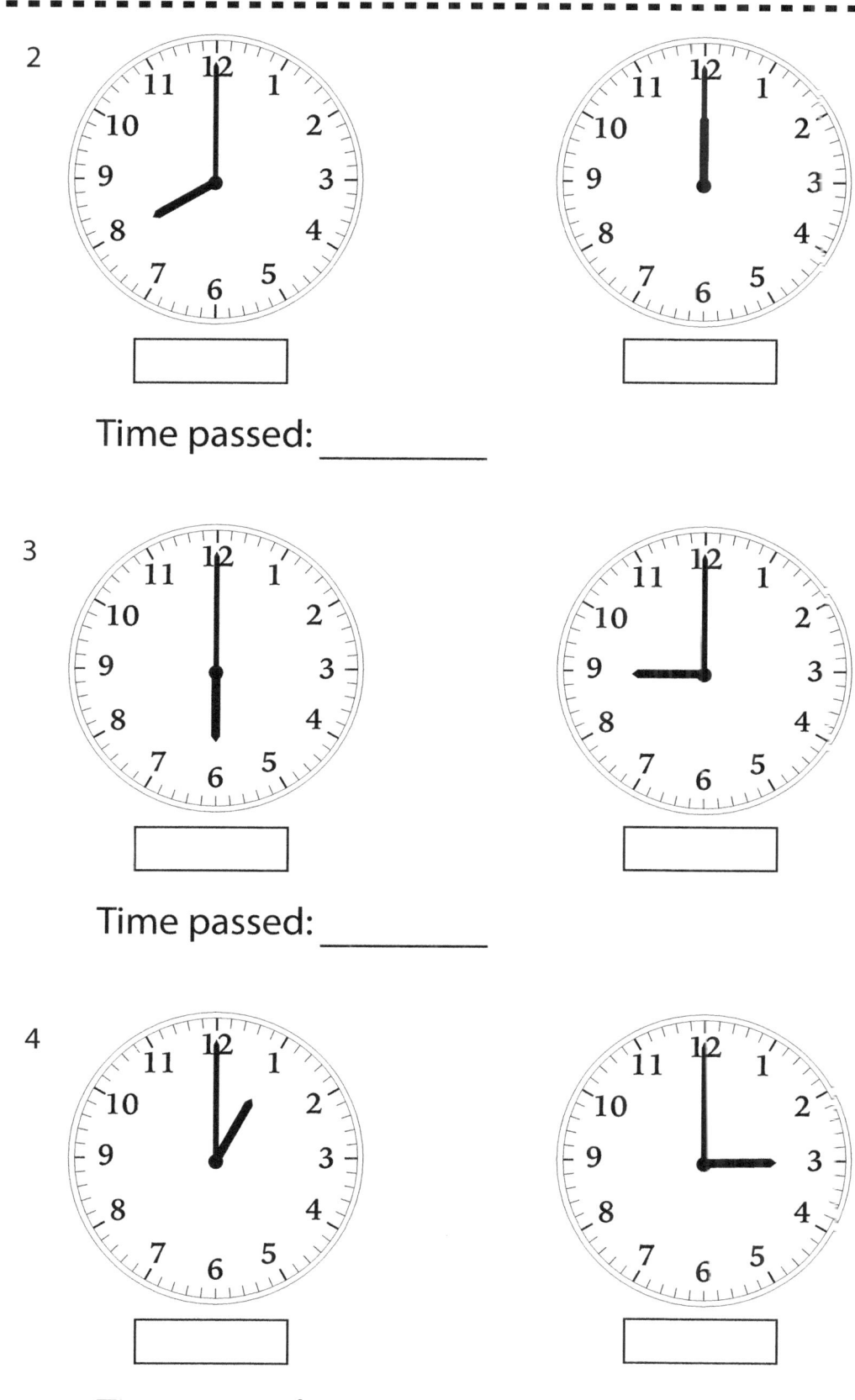

2

Time passed: _____

3

Time passed: _____

4

Time passed: _____

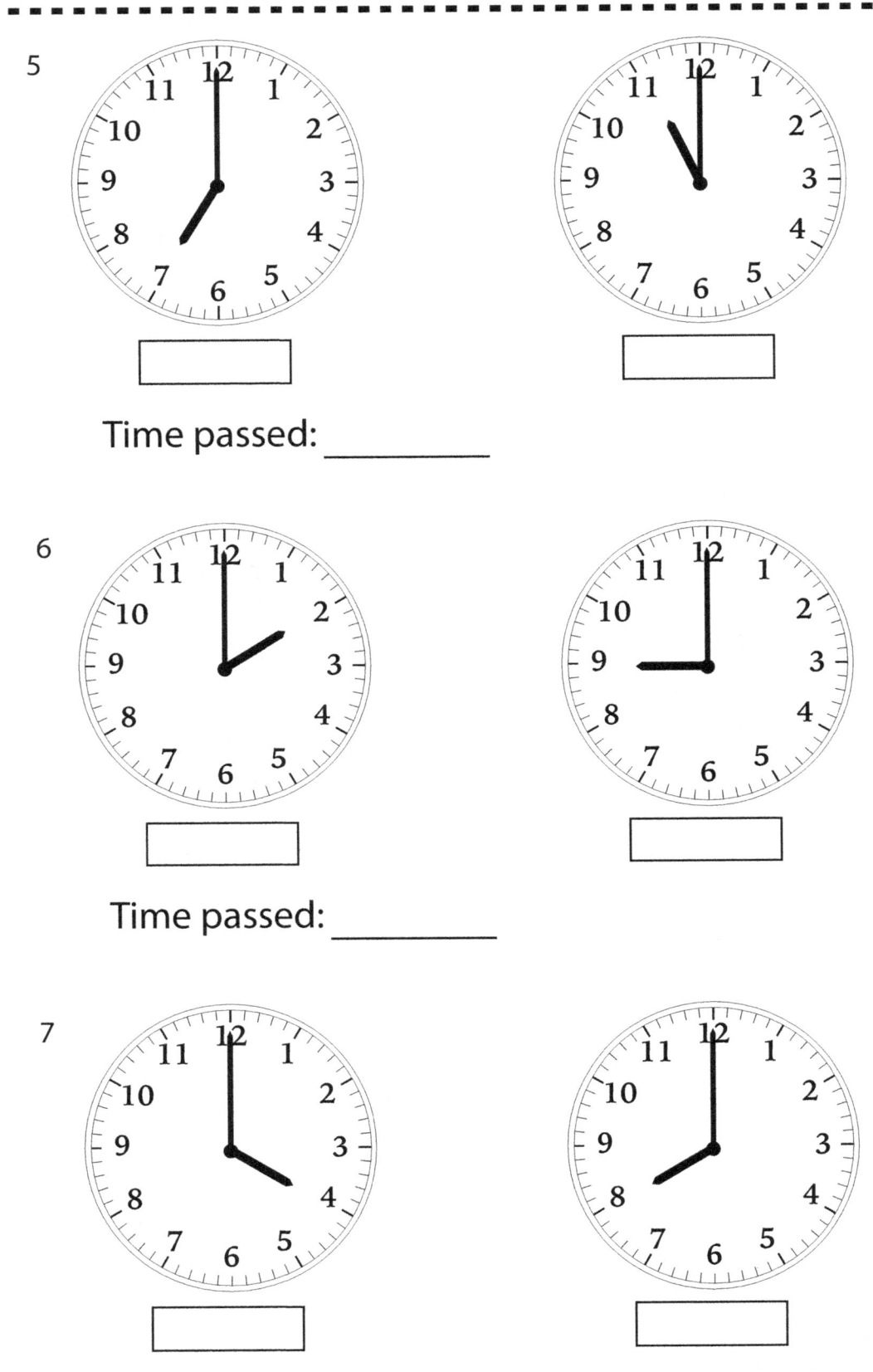

5

Time passed: _____

6

Time passed: _____

7

Time passed: _____

22

Word Problems with Hours

1. Billy starts his lunch at noon (12:00). He finishes lunch at 1:00. How long was his lunch?

Answer: _____

2. Sasha starts his movie at 3:00 and it ends at 5:00. How long was the movie?

Answer: _____

3. Danielle drives in her car from 8:00 to 3:00. How many hours did she drive?

Answer: _____

23

Word Problems with Hours

4. Liam goes to school at 9:00 and gets home at 3:00. How long was he at school?

Answer: _____

5. Henry goes to sleep at 8:00 and wakes up at 6:00. How many hours did he sleep?

Answer: _____

6. Raymond starts to watch TV at 5:00 and finishes at 8:00. How many hours did he watch TV?

Answer: _____

Word Problems with Hours

7. Emma goes to school at 8:00 and gets home at 4:00. How long was she at school?

Answer: _____

8. Lizzie starts playing with her friend at 3:00 and stops at 6:00. How long did she play with her friend?

Answer: _____

9. Kyle starts writing a story at 5:00 and finishes it at 7:00. How many hours did he spend writing?

Answer: _____

Half Hours and Quarter Hours

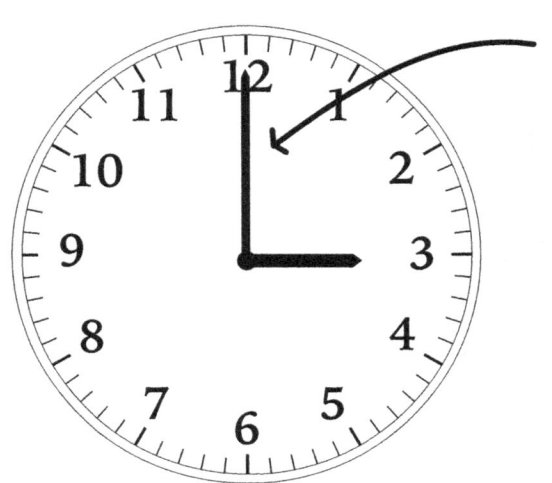

This is called the minute hand! The minute hand is smaller and longer than the hour hand.

How many minutes are in an hour?

Count each of the black little lines that go all the way around the clock. Write the total here: _____

Did you count 60 black lines? That means there are **60** minutes in one hour!

Look at the clock below:

The Minute Hand:

When the minute hand moves from the 12 to the 6, that means that **30 minutes** have passed.

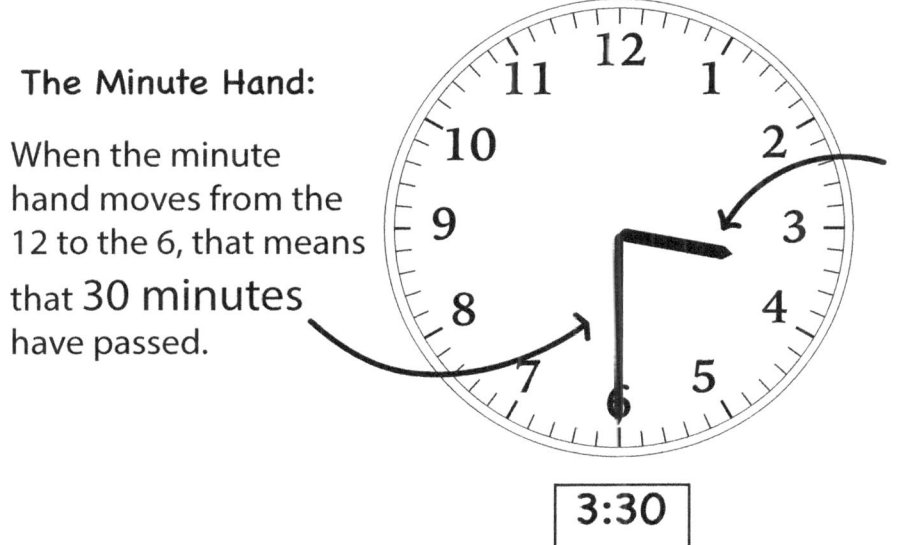

3:30

The Hour Hand:

As the minute hand moves around the clock, the hour hand slowly moves from one number to the next.

Draw in the hour hand pointing halfway in between the 4 and the 5. Then draw the minute hand pointing to the 6. This is how you show 4:30.

Draw in the hour hand pointing halfway in between the 12 and the 1. Then draw the minute hand pointing to the 6. This is how you show 12:30

Circle the Correct Time

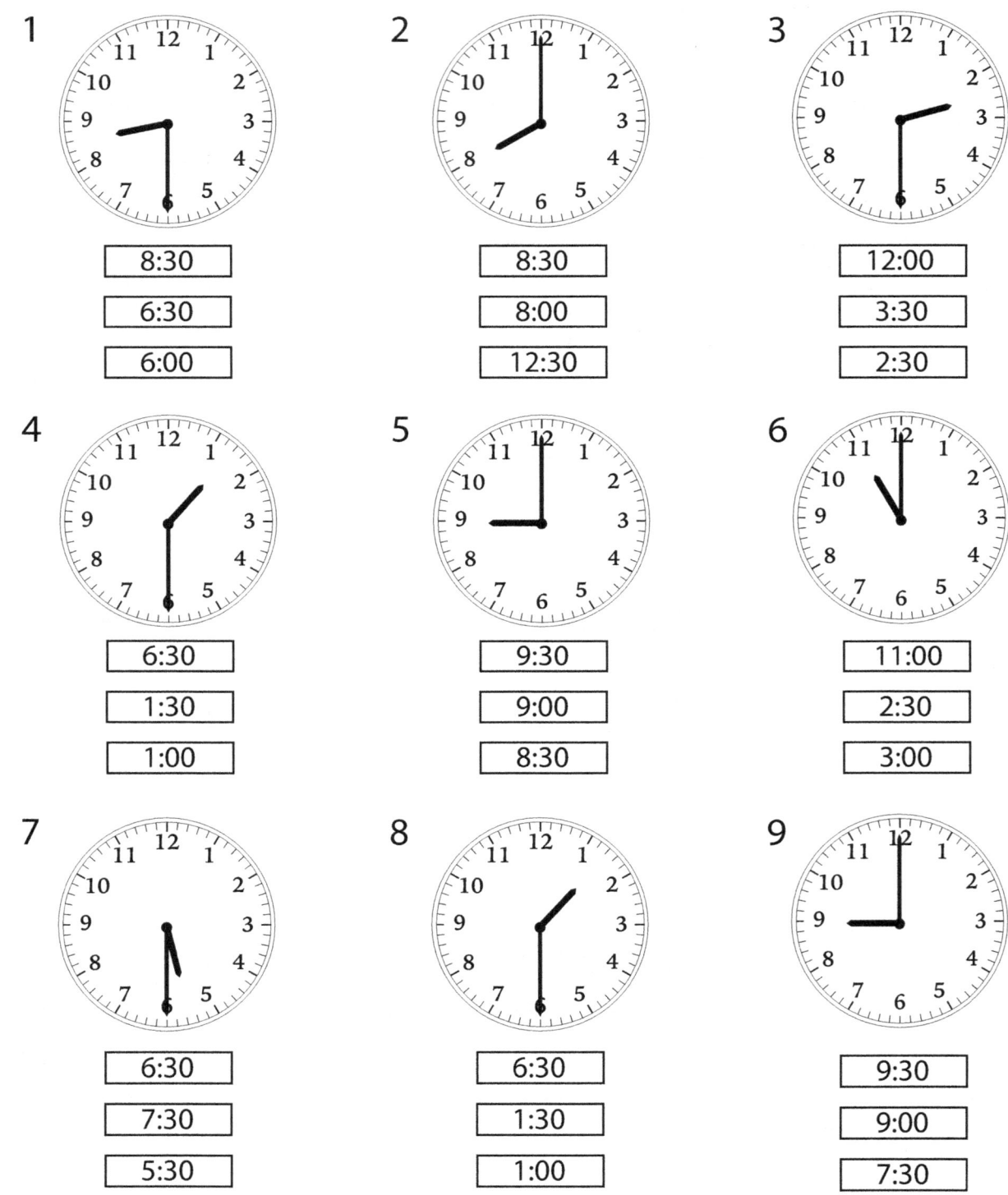

1

8:30

6:30

6:00

2

8:30

8:00

12:30

3

12:00

3:30

2:30

4

6:30

1:30

1:00

5

9:30

9:00

8:30

6

11:00

2:30

3:00

7

6:30

7:30

5:30

8

6:30

1:30

1:00

9

9:30

9:00

7:30

Circle the Correct Time

10

12:30

6:30

6:00

11

4:00

3:30

3:00

12

2:00

3:30

2:30

13

10:30

1:30

11:00

14

7:30

9:00

7:00

15

11:30

12:30

11:00

16

6:00

2:30

6:30

17

3:30

3:00

6:30

18

2:30

1:00

12:00

Circle the Correct Time

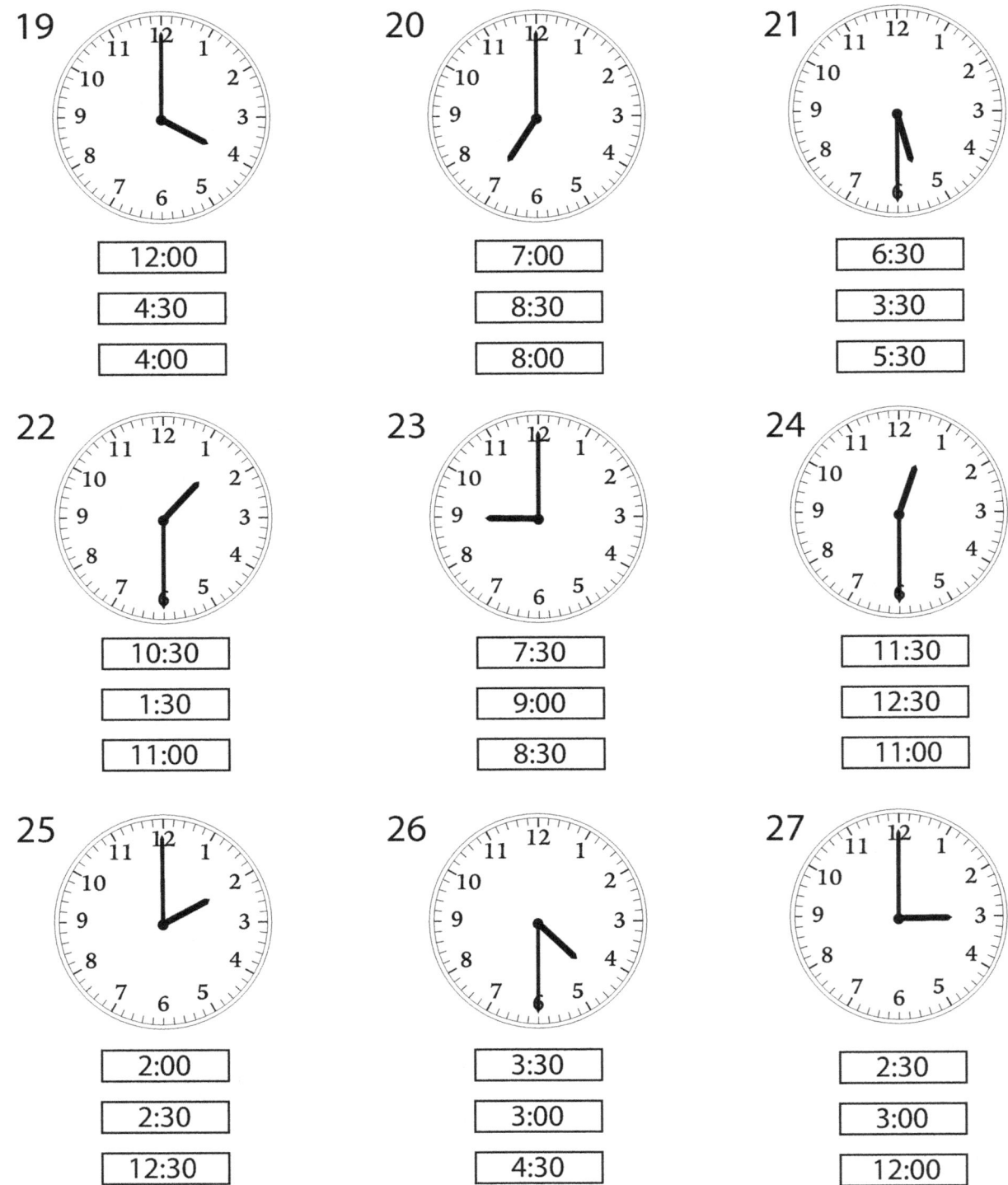

19

12:00
4:30
4:00

20

7:00
8:30
8:00

21

6:30
3:30
5:30

22

10:30
1:30
11:00

23

7:30
9:00
8:30

24

11:30
12:30
11:00

25

2:00
2:30
12:30

26

3:30
3:00
4:30

27

2:30
3:00
12:00

30

Write in the Correct Time

1

_____

2

_____

3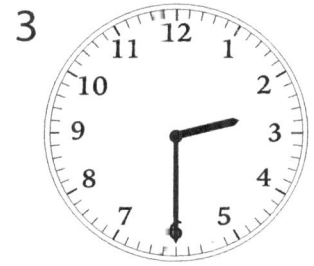

_____

4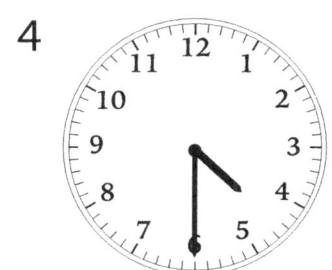

_____

5

_____

6

_____

7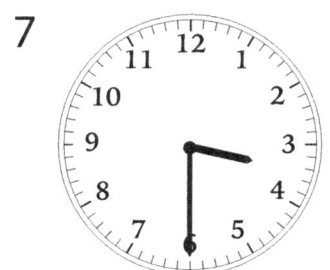

_____

8

_____

9

_____

Write in the Correct Time

10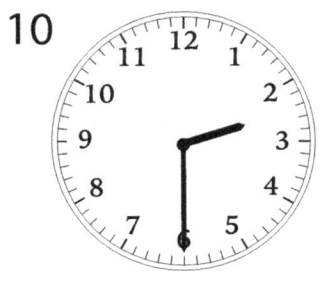

_____

11

_____

12

_____

13

_____

14

_____

15

_____

16

_____

17

_____

18

_____

Write in the Correct Time

19

_____

20

_____

21

_____

22

_____

23

_____

24

_____

25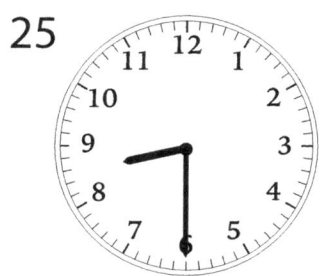

_____

26

_____

27

_____

33

Draw the hands on the clock

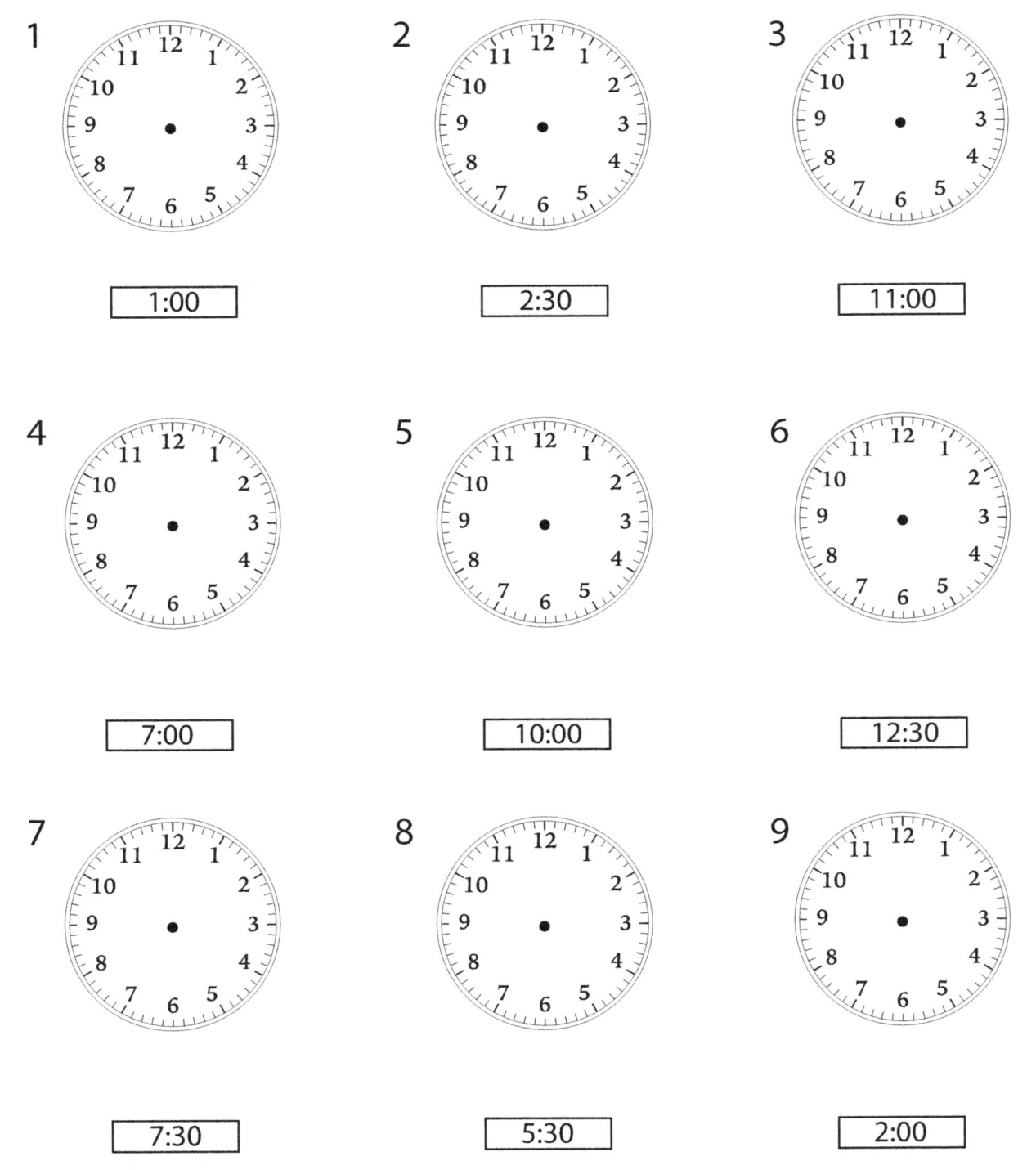

1   1:00

2   2:30

3   11:00

4   7:00

5   10:00

6   12:30

7   7:30

8   5:30

9   2:00

Draw the hands on the clock

10

3:30

11

10:30

12

6:00

13

1:00

14

9:30

15

10:30

16

5:30

17

7:30

18

6:00

Draw the hands on the clock

19   4:30

20   12:30

21   11:00

22   9:00

23   4:00

24   5:00

25   3:30

26   9:30

27   10:00

Quarter Hours

An hour can be divided into 4 equal parts!

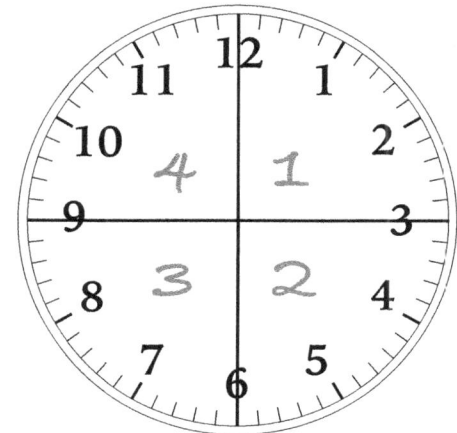

It might help to think about a pie or pizza being cut into four pieces like this!

Count the black lines in each section. There are 15! That means that a quarter hour is 15 minutes long.

| 4:00 | 4:15 | 4:30 | 4:45 |

Look at the hour hand when the clock says 4:00. Now look at the hour hand when the clock says 4:45. What do you notice?

Remember when the minute hand moves around the clock, the hour hand moves slowly in between the two big numbers!

Circle the Correct Time

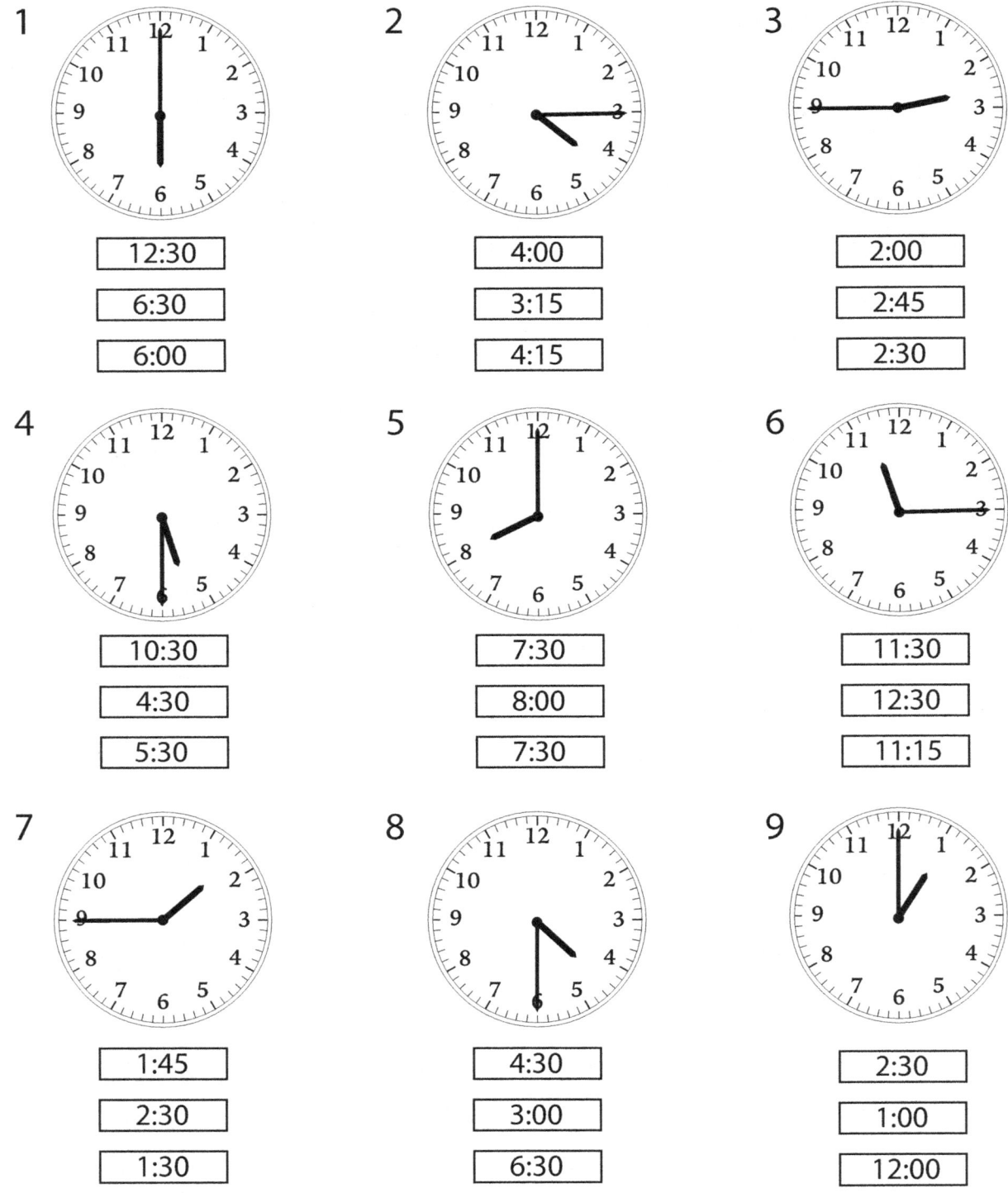

1

12:30
6:30
6:00

2

4:00
3:15
4:15

3

2:00
2:45
2:30

4

10:30
4:30
5:30

5

7:30
8:00
7:30

6

11:30
12:30
11:15

7

1:45
2:30
1:30

8

4:30
3:00
6:30

9

2:30
1:00
12:00

Circle the Correct Time

10

12:30

6:30

3:00

11

4:00

3:15

8:30

12

7:00

7 45

7:30

13

5:15

4:15

5:30

14

1:00

1:15

2:30

15

5:30

4:30

5:15

16

6:45

6:30

9:30

17

4:30

3:00

2:30

18

7:45

7:00

9:00

Circle the Correct Time

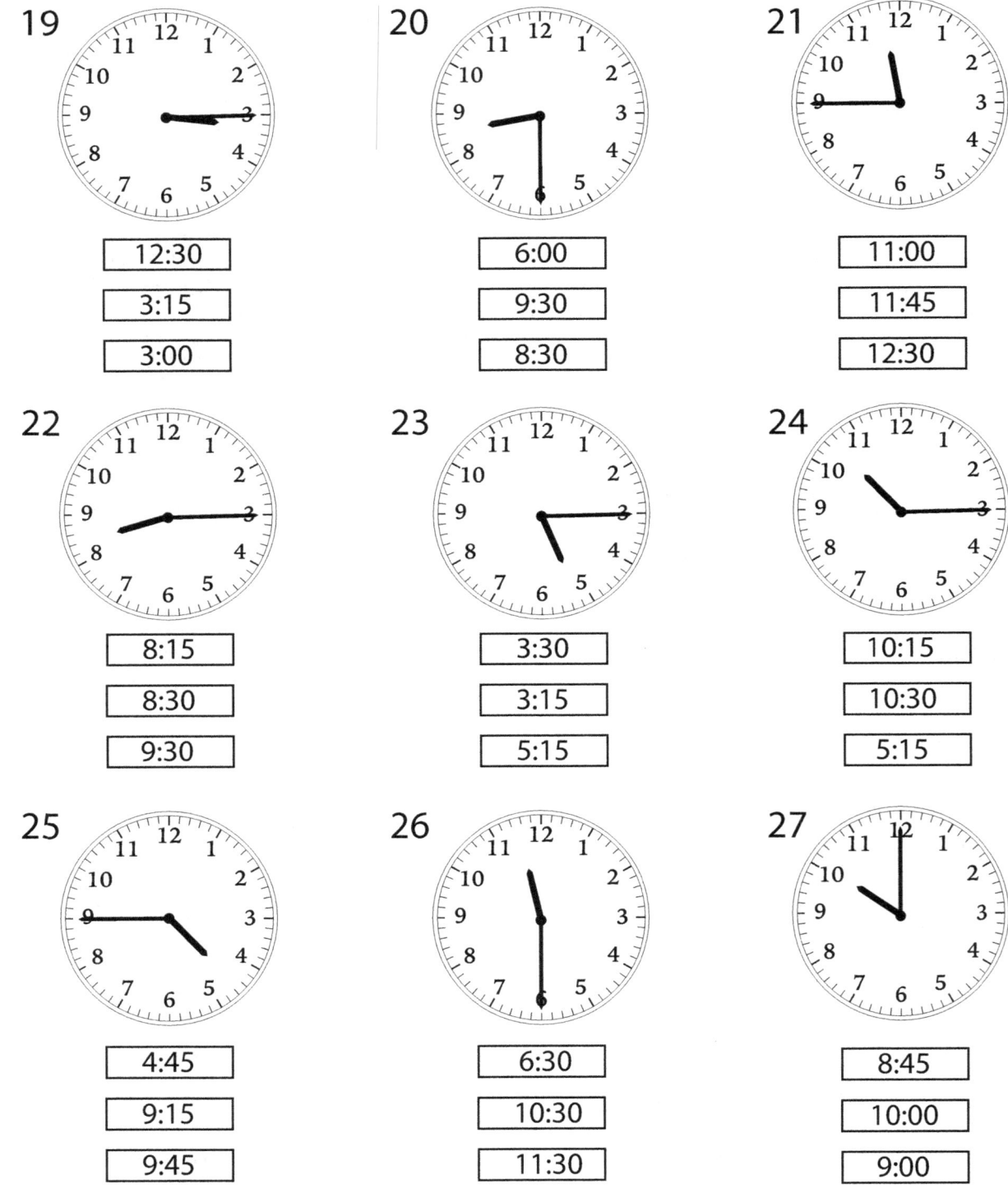

19
12:30
3:15
3:00

20
6:00
9:30
8:30

21
11:00
11:45
12:30

22
8:15
8:30
9:30

23
3:30
3:15
5:15

24
10:15
10:30
5:15

25
4:45
9:15
9:45

26
6:30
10:30
11:30

27
8:45
10:00
9:00

Write in the Correct Time

1
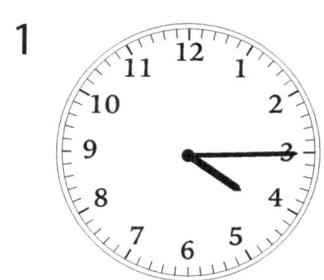

_____

2

_____

3

_____

4

_____

5

_____

6

_____

7
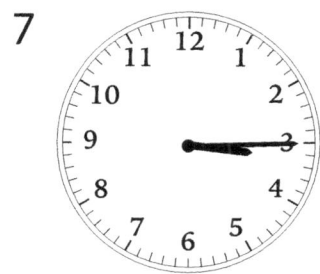

_____

8
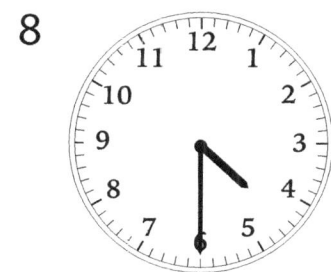

_____

9

_____

Write in the Correct Time

10

_____

11

_____

12

_____

13

_____

14

_____

15

_____

16

_____

17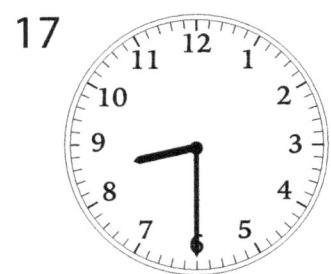

_____

18

_____

Write in the Correct Time

19

_____

20

_____

21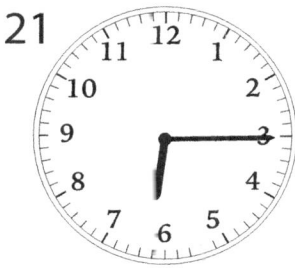

_____

22

_____

23

_____

24

_____

25

_____

26

_____

27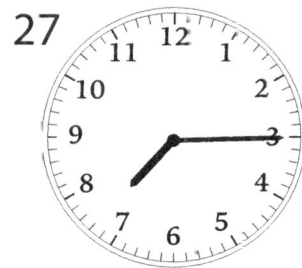

_____

Draw the hands on the clock

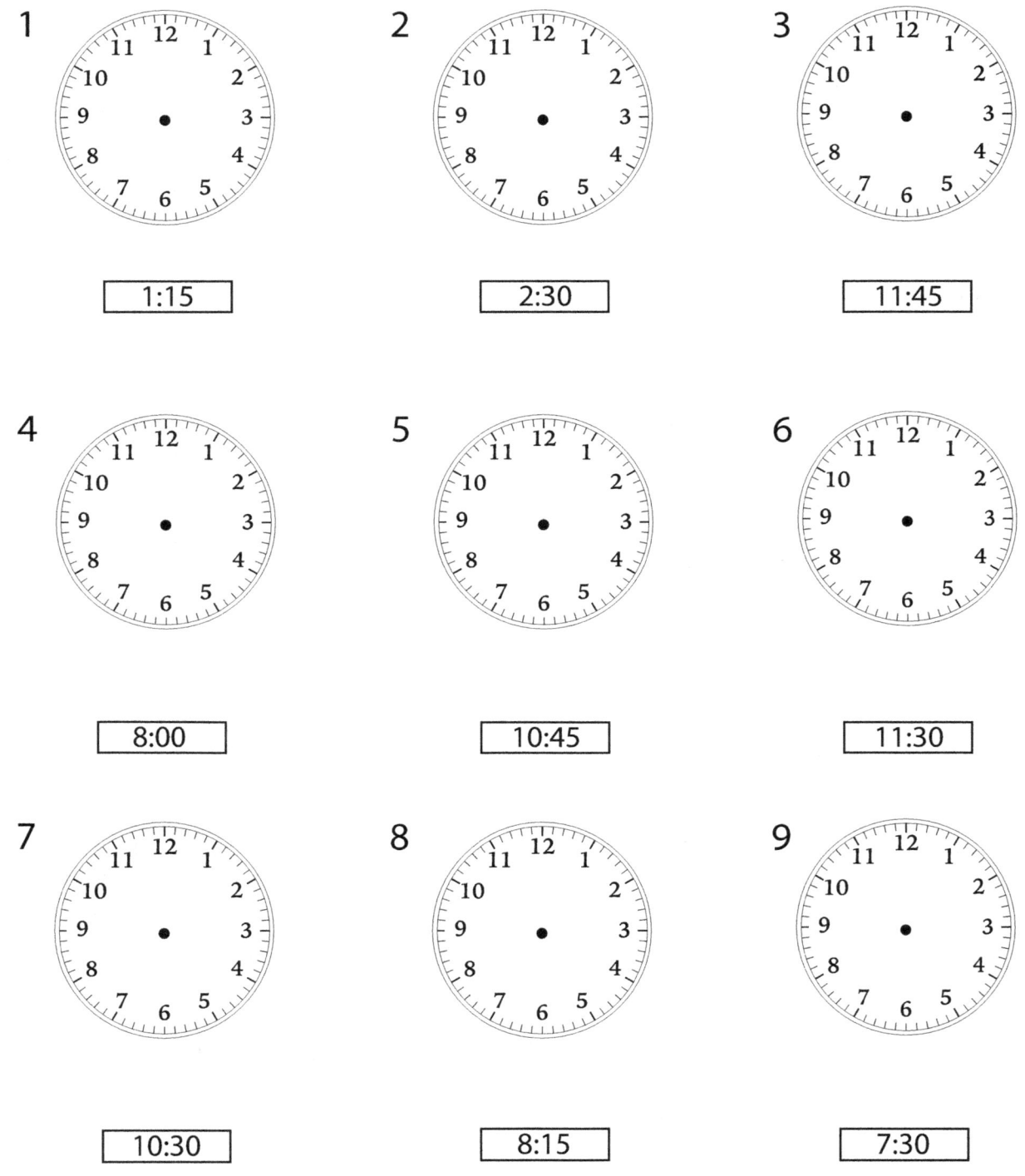

1 1:15

2 2:30

3 11:45

4 8:00

5 10:45

6 11:30

7 10:30

8 8:15

9 7:30

Draw the hands on the clock

10

1:30

11

2:15

12

9:15

13

1:30

14

11:15

15

9:45

16

10:30

17

7:15

18

6:00

Draw the hands on the clock

19   2:15

20   11:30

21   11:45

22   3:00

23   4:15

24   10:00

25   3:30

26   6:45

27   12:00

How much time has passed?

Look at the clocks and write in the time. How many minutes have passed?

Example:

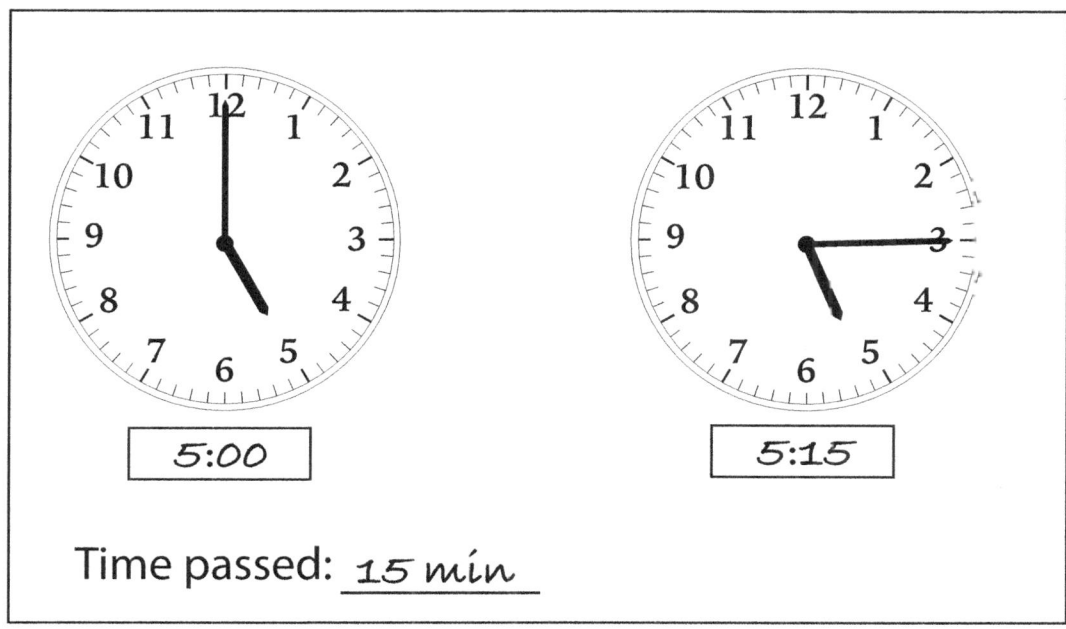

5:00

5:15

Time passed: __15 min__

1

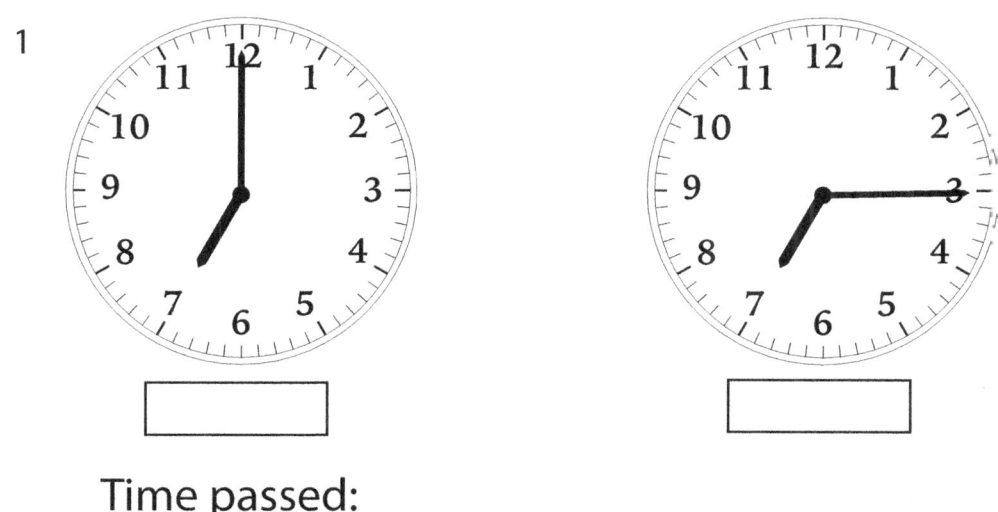

Time passed: _____

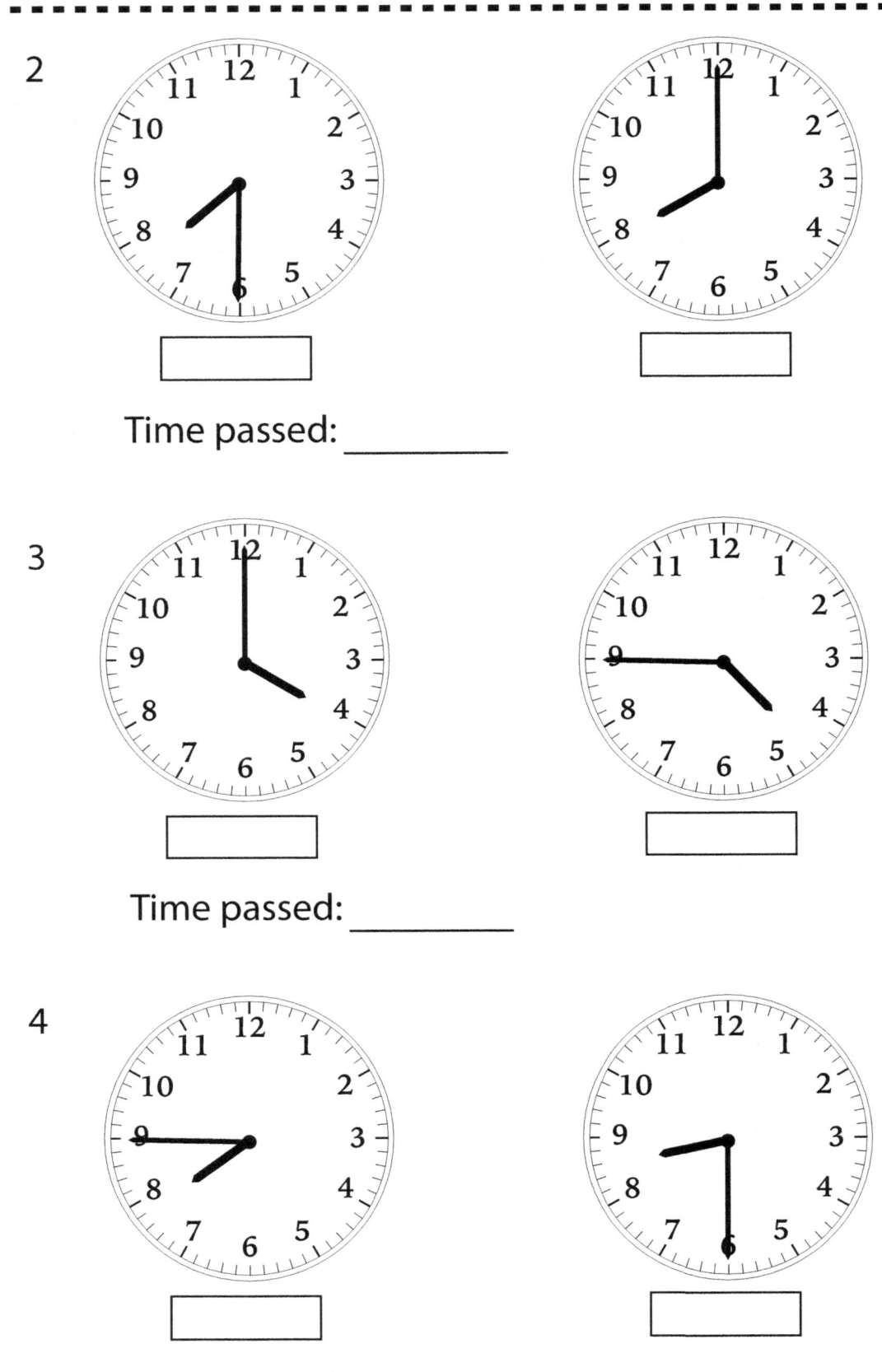

2

Time passed: _____

3

Time passed: _____

4

Time passed: _____

Word Problems with Quarter and Half Hours

1. Leo starts his lunch at noon (12:00). He finishes lunch at 12:45. How long was his lunch?

Answer: _____

2. Lilly starts her math test at 3:00 and finishes at 3:30. How long did she work on her test?

Answer: _____

3. Brandon starts his run at 8:45 and stops at 9:15. How long did he run?

Answer: _____

Word Problems with Hours

4. Saoirse was at the grocery store from 4:15 to 4:45. How long was she at the store?

Answer: _____

5. Micah takes a nap from 2:30 to 3:15. How long did he sleep?

Answer: _____

6. Mara leaves for her walk at 5:00 and gets home at 5:15. How long was she walking?

Answer: _____

Telling Time up to Five Minutes

Do you know how to skip count by 5's? Counting by 5's will help us learn to tell time.

Fill in the blanks:

Count how many black lines there are between number 1 and number 2 on this clock:

There are 5! This means that each big number represents 5 minutes.

Skip count by 5's to fill in the blanks around the clock.

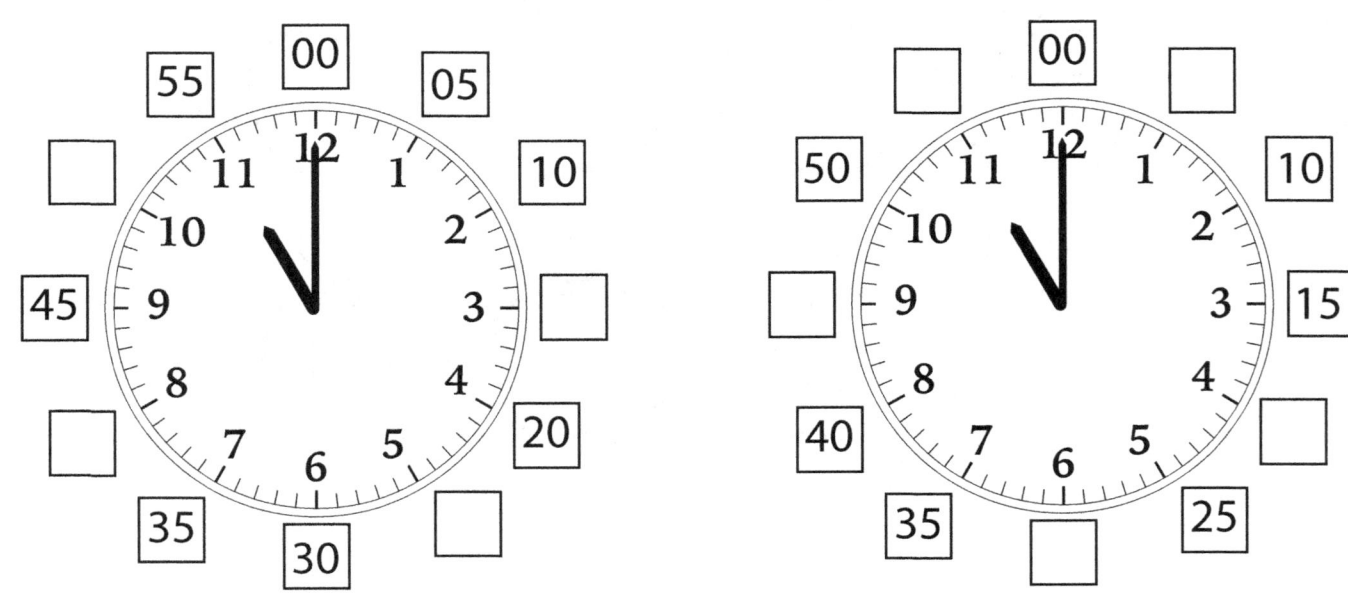

Write in what time it is. Use skip counting to help you.

Example:

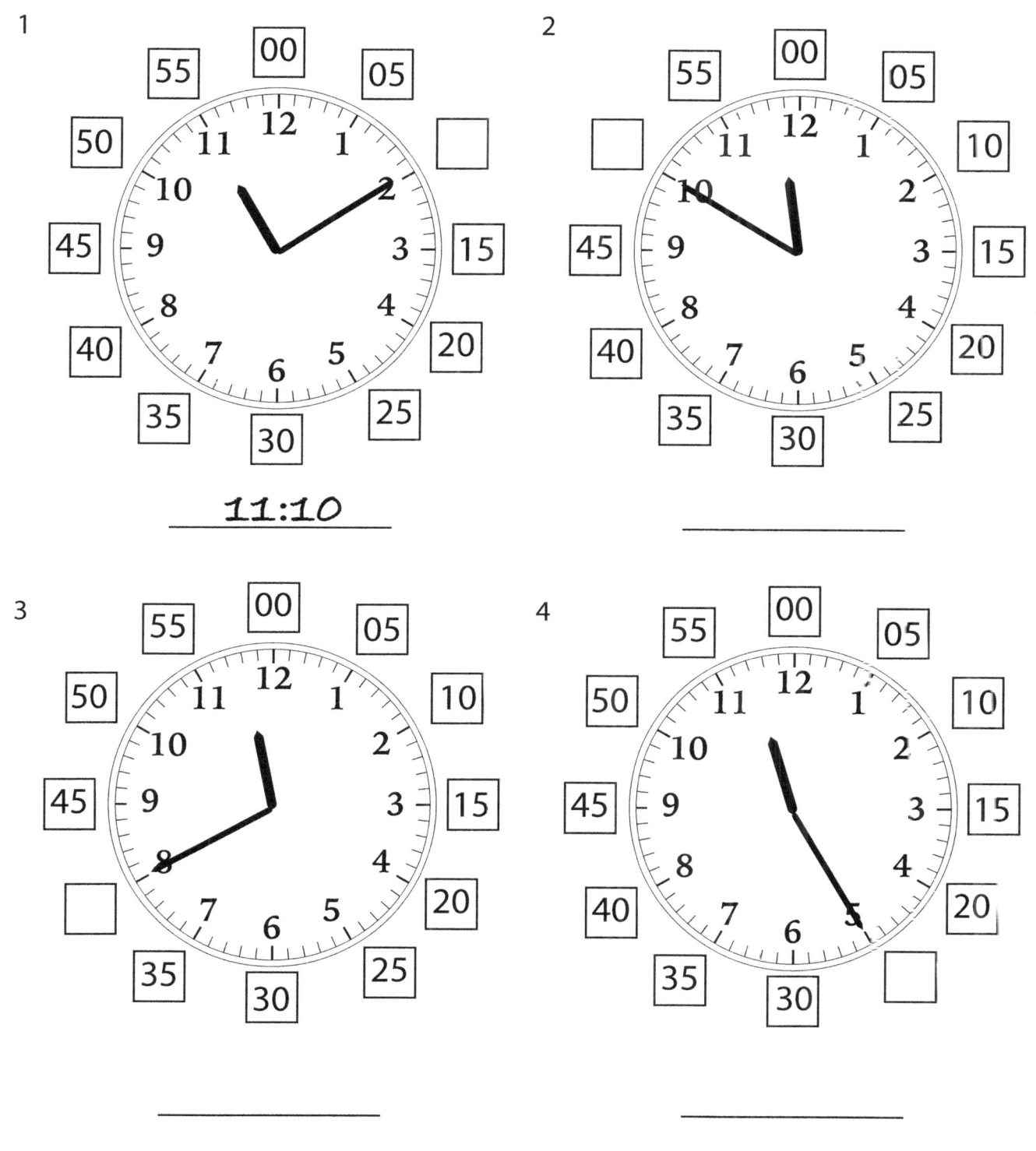

1

<u>   11:10   </u>

2

_____

3

_____

4

_____

Circle the Correct Time

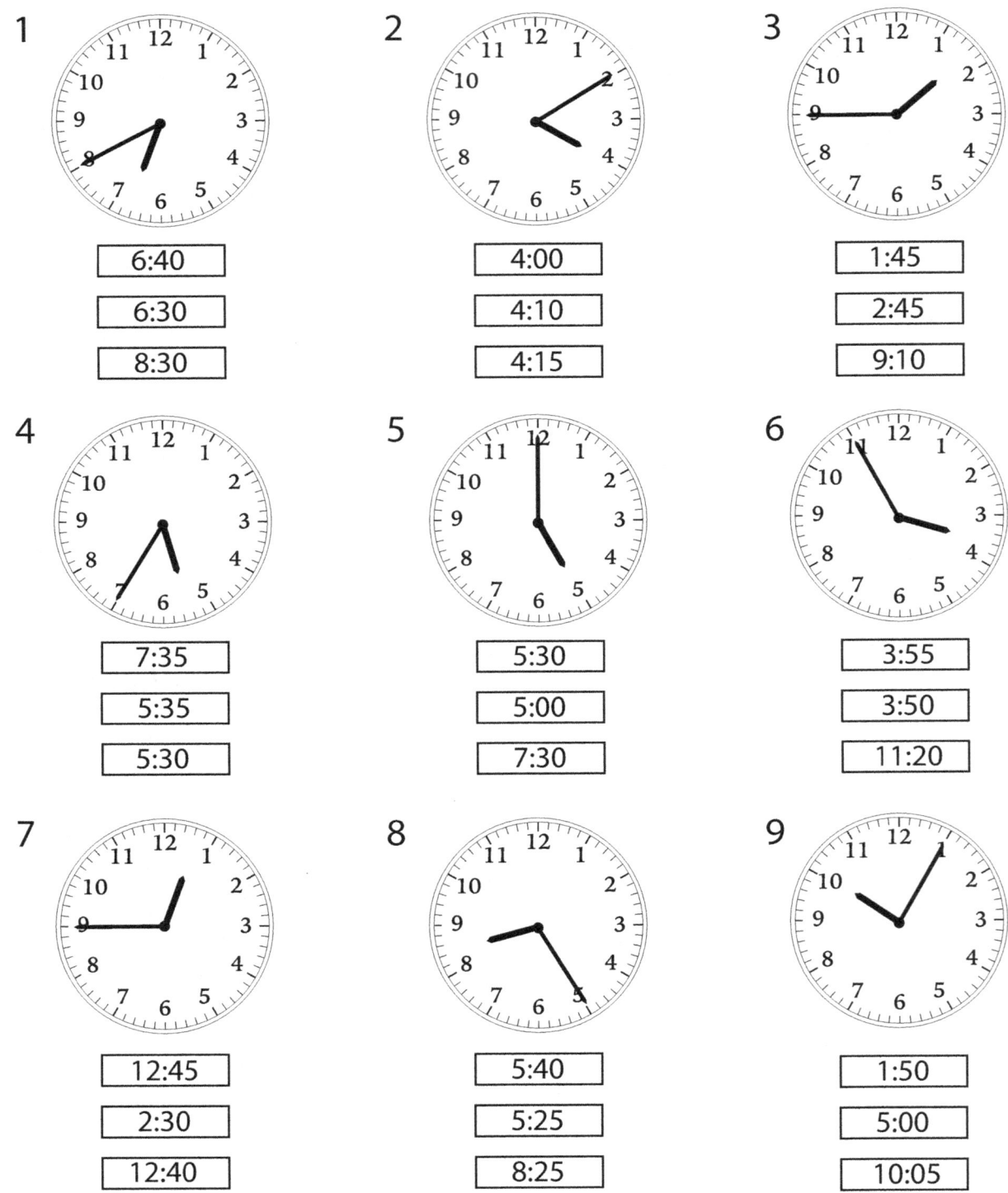

1
6:40
6:30
8:30

2
4:00
4:10
4:15

3
1:45
2:45
9:10

4
7:35
5:35
5:30

5
5:30
5:00
7:30

6
3:55
3:50
11:20

7
12:45
2:30
12:40

8
5:40
5:25
8:25

9
1:50
5:00
10:05

Circle the Correct Time

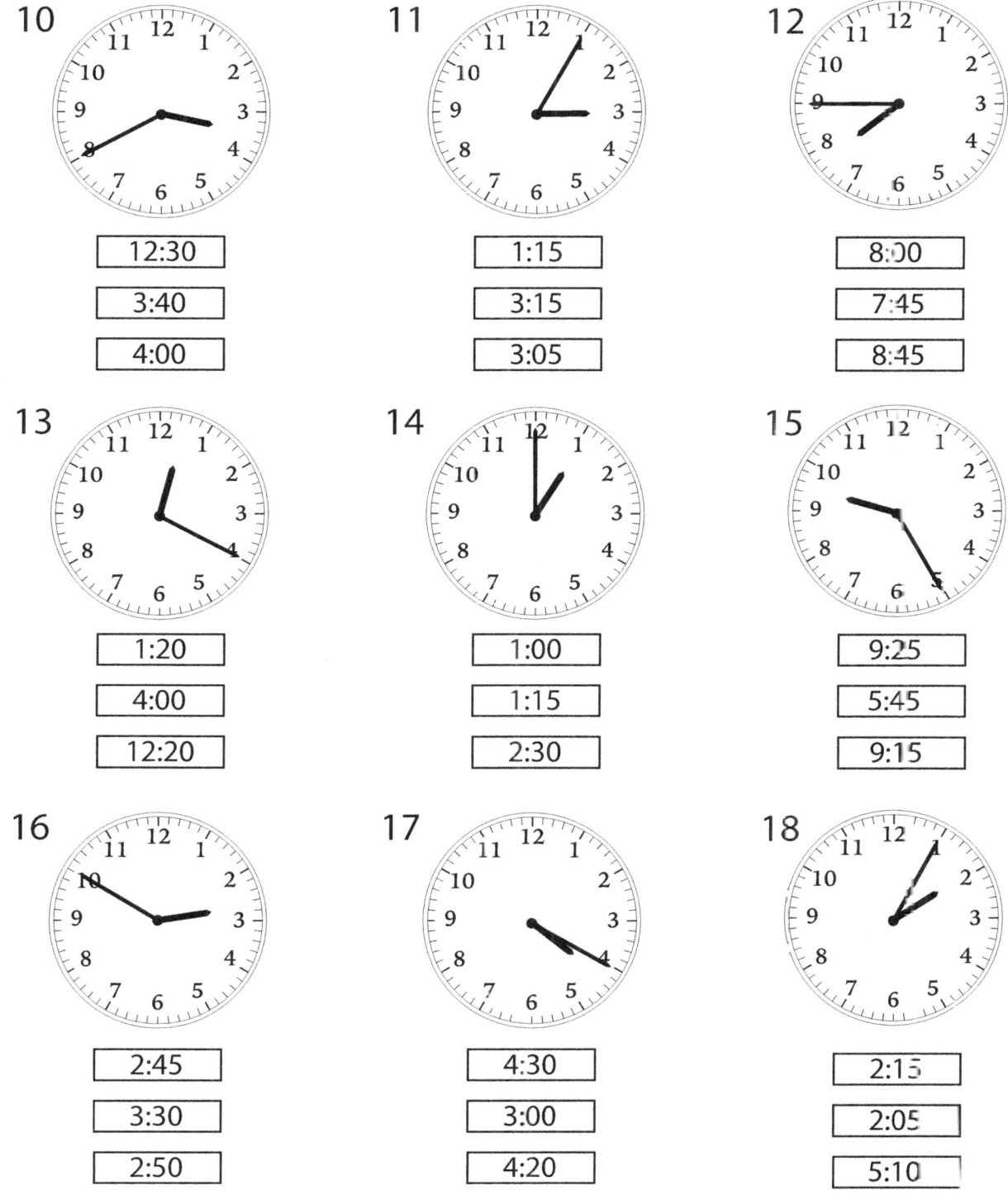

10

12:30

3:40

4:00

11

1:15

3:15

3:05

12

8:00

7:45

8:45

13

1:20

4:00

12:20

14

1:00

1:15

2:30

15

9:25

5:45

9:15

16

2:45

3:30

2:50

17

4:30

3:00

4:20

18

2:15

2:05

5:10

Circle the Correct Time

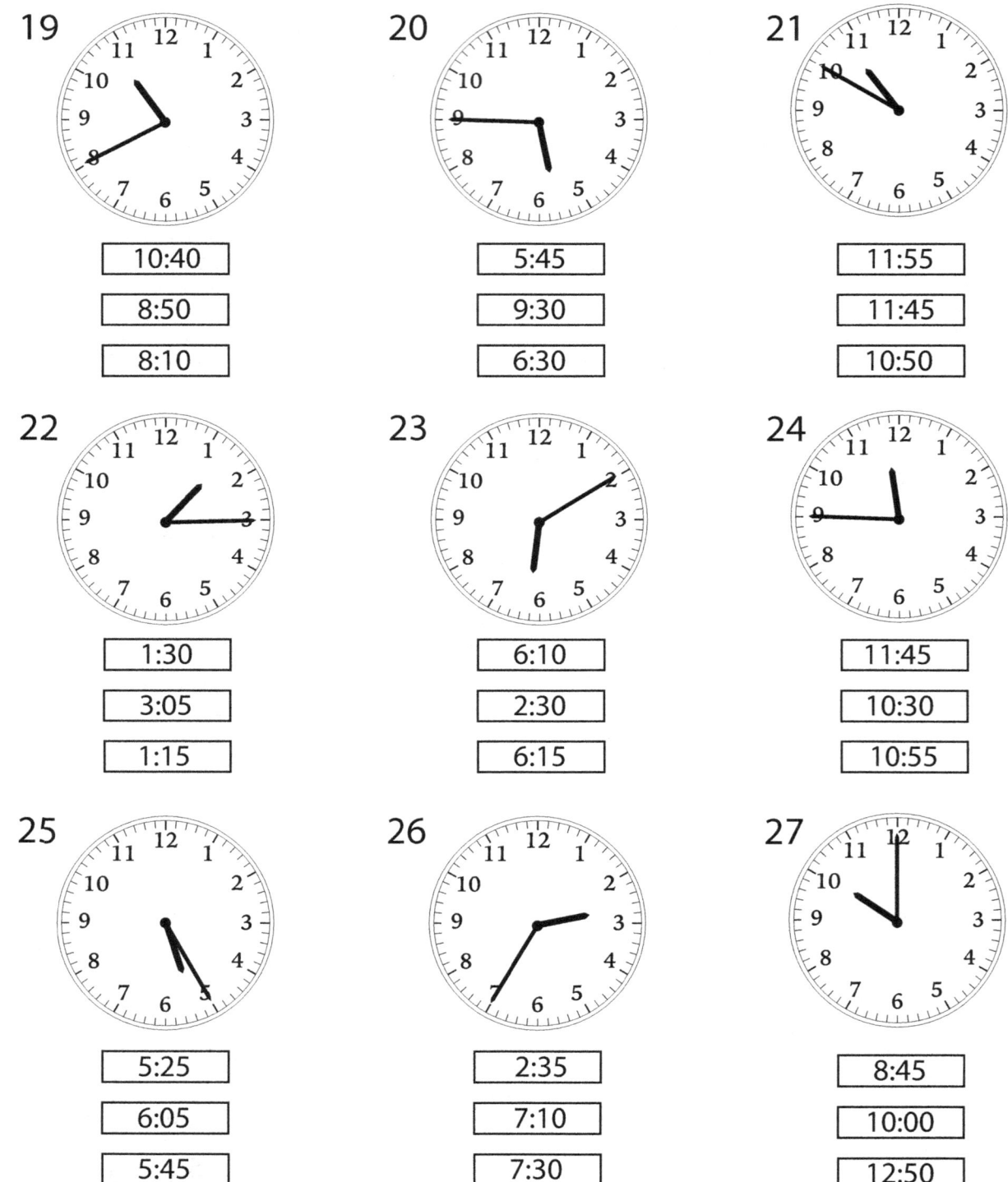

19

10:40

8:50

8:10

20

5:45

9:30

6:30

21

11:55

11:45

10:50

22

1:30

3:05

1:15

23

6:10

2:30

6:15

24

11:45

10:30

10:55

25

5:25

6:05

5:45

26

2:35

7:10

7:30

27

8:45

10:00

12:50

Draw a line to connect the clock with the correct time

1

2

3

4

9:10

7:45

1:15

6:30

Draw a line to connect the clock with the correct time

5

4:40

6

3:45

7

11:25

8

12:55

58

Draw a line to connect the clock with the correct time

9

                       9:15

10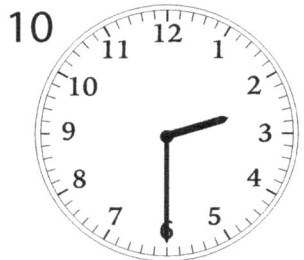

                       12:55

11

                       2:30

12

                       2:20

Write in the Correct Time

1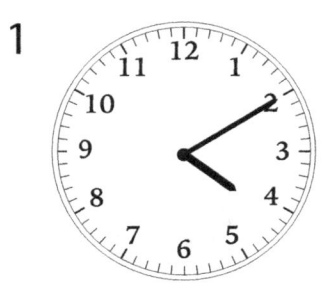

_____

2

_____

3

_____

4

_____

5

_____

6

_____

7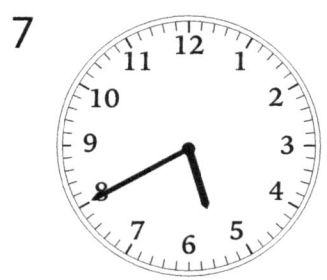

_____

8

_____

9

_____

Write in the Correct Time

10

_____

11

_____

12

_____

13

_____

14

_____

15

_____

16

_____

17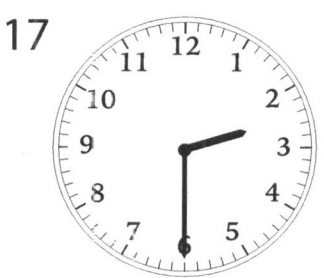

_____

18

_____

Write in the Correct Time

19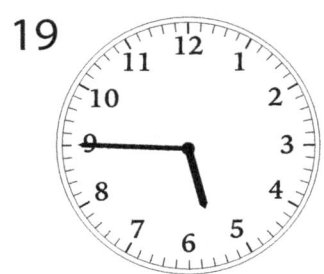

_____

20

_____

21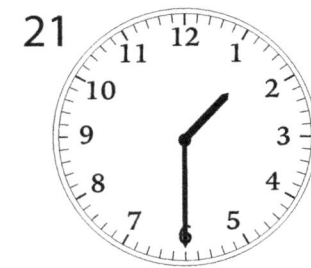

_____

22

_____

23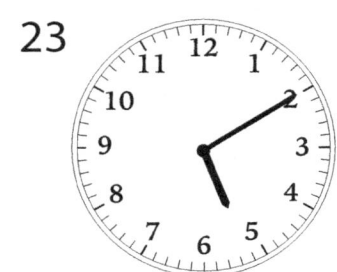

_____

24

_____

25

_____

26

_____

27

_____

Draw the hands on the clock

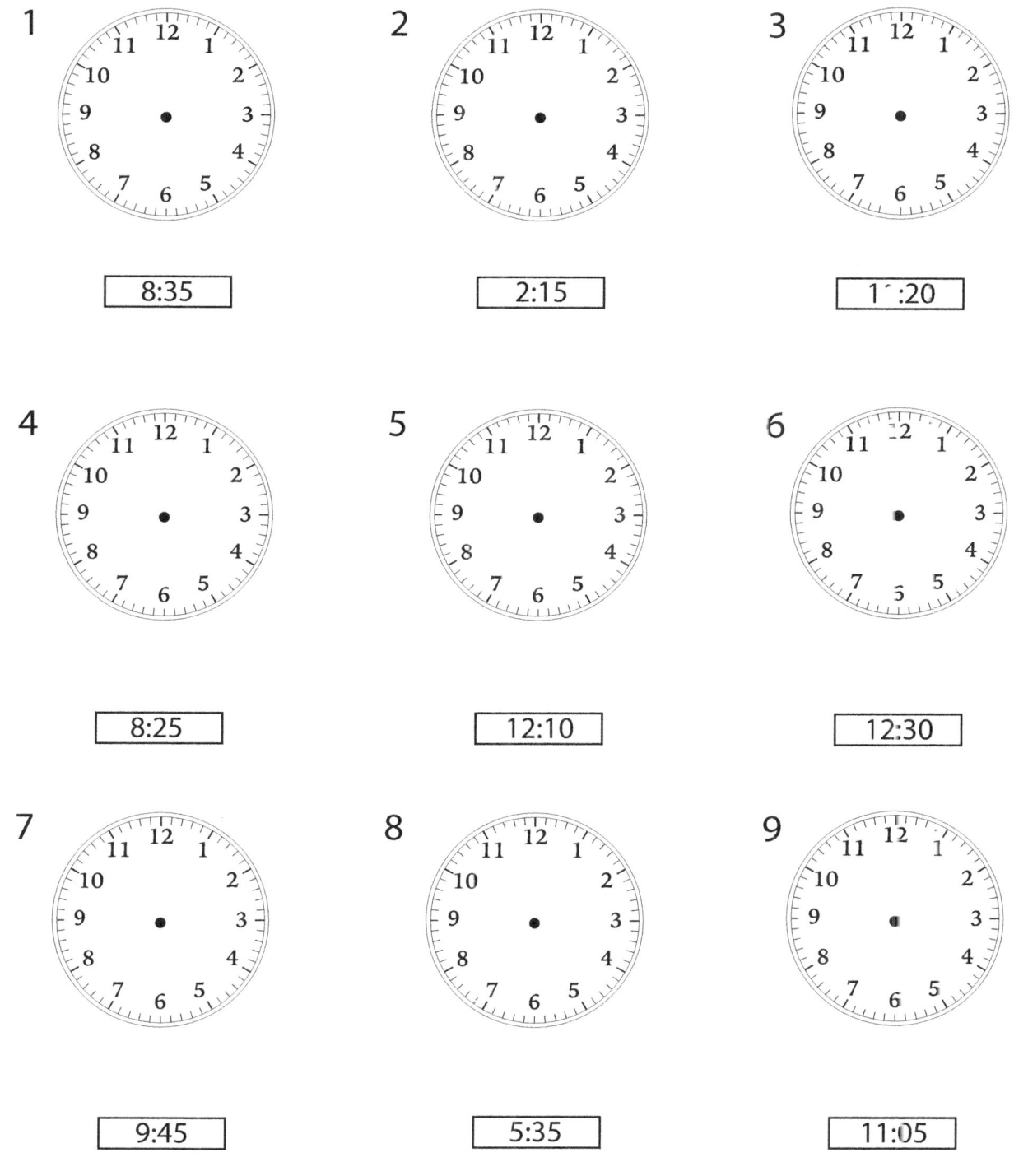

1   8:35

2   2:15

3   1˙:20

4   8:25

5   12:10

6   12:30

7   9:45

8   5:35

9   11:05

Draw the hands on the clock

10   8:10

11   7:25

12   11:30

13   1:55

14   8:20

15   10:05

16   3:05

17   2:35

18   6:05

Draw the hands on the clock

19

3:45

20

10:20

21

7:05

22

9:40

23

4:40

24

8:25

25

9:10

26

7:50

27

8:20

How much time has passed?

Look at the clocks and write in the time. How many minutes have passed?

Example:

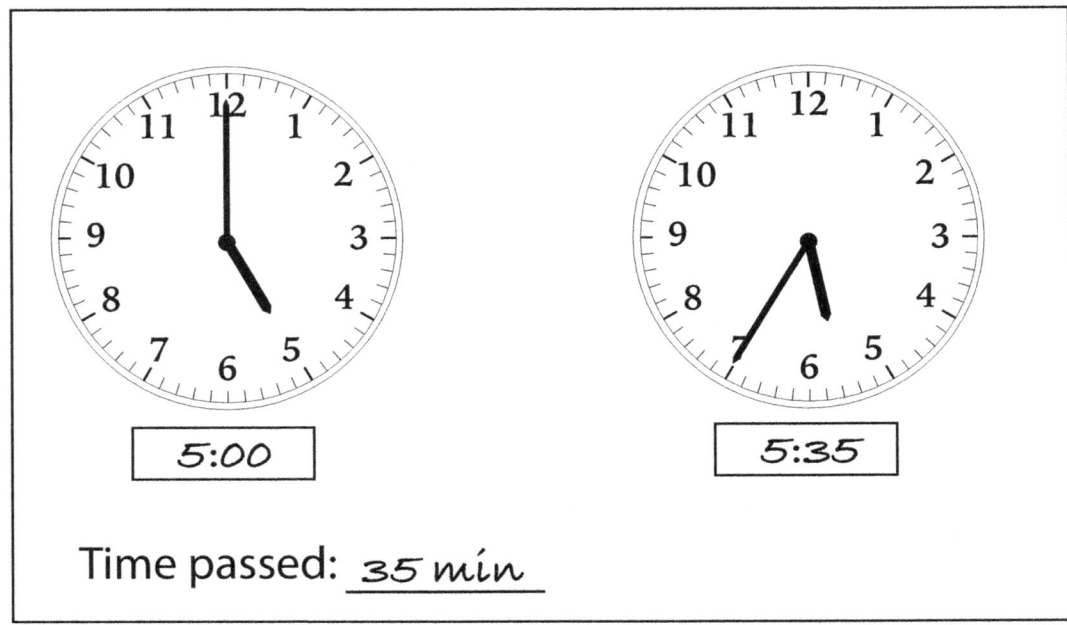

5:00

5:35

Time passed: _35 min_

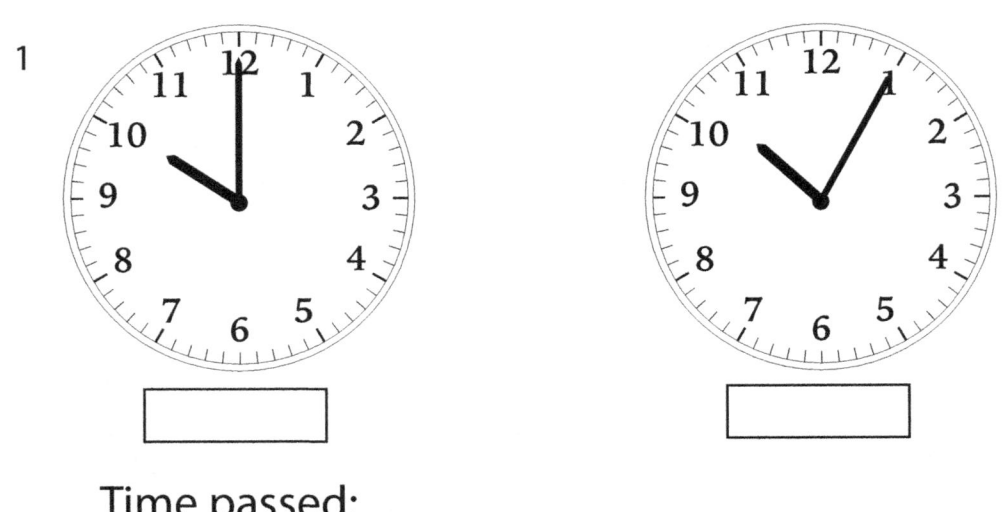

1

Time passed: _____

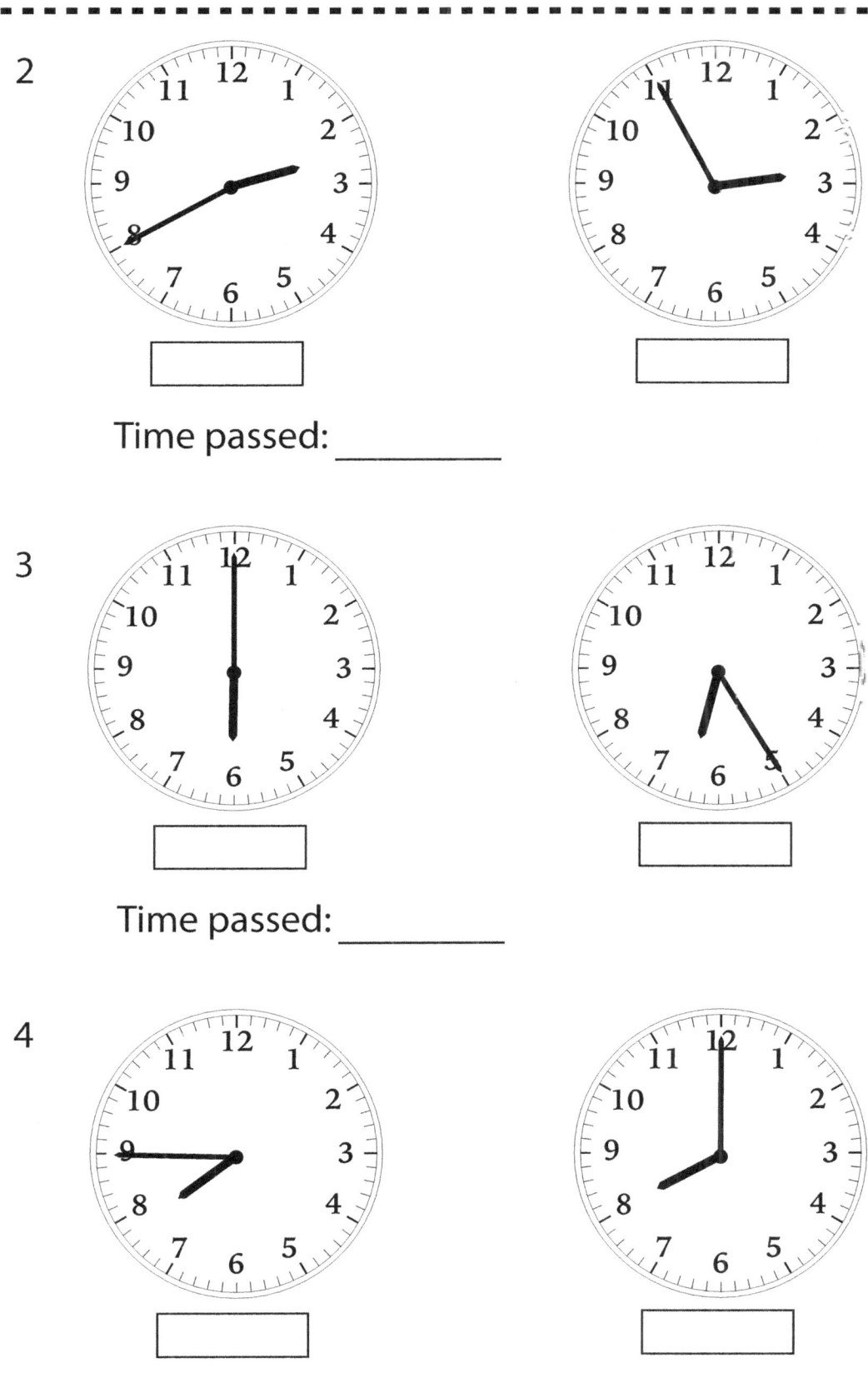

2

Time passed: _____

3

Time passed: _____

4

Time passed: _____

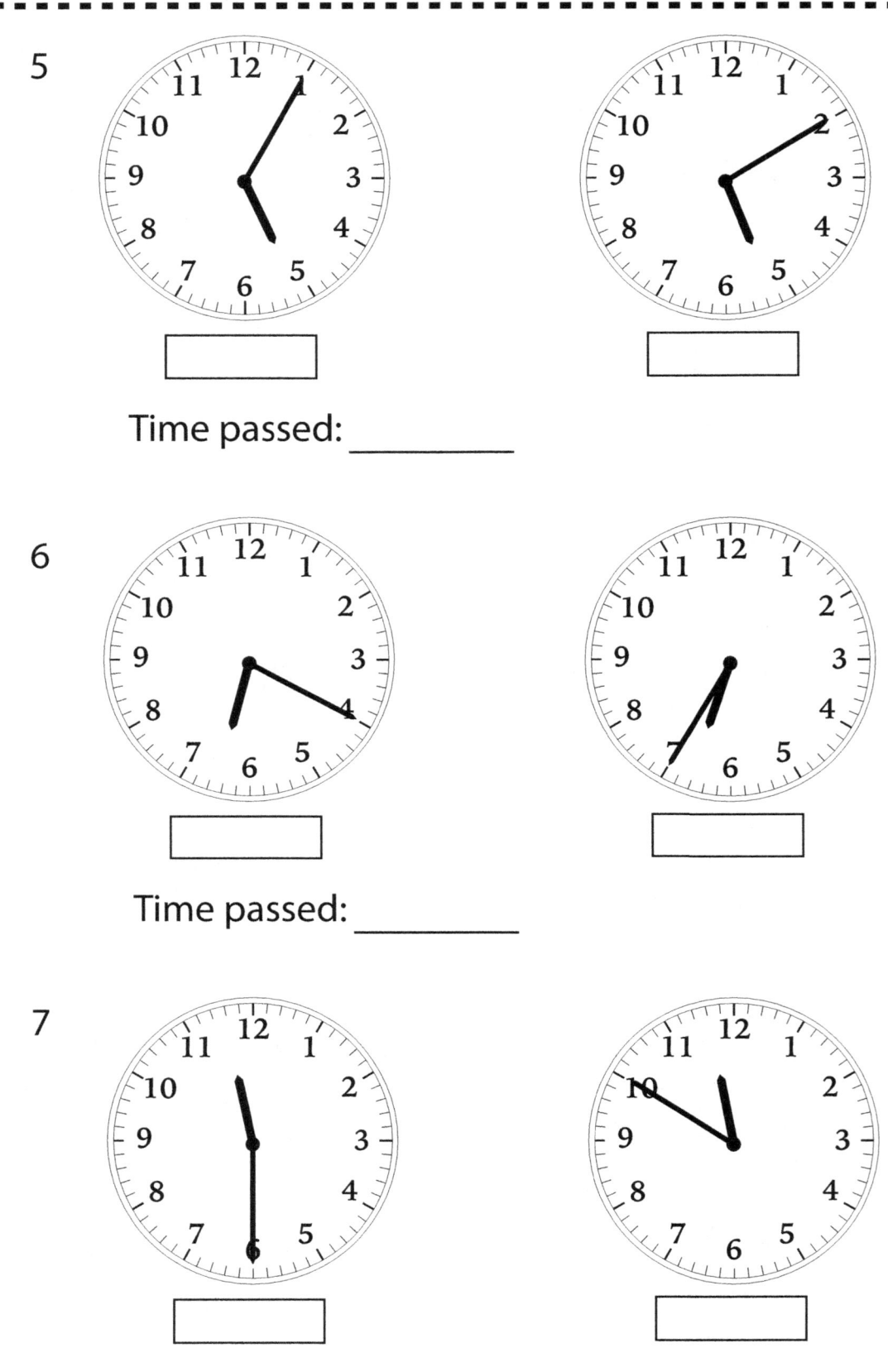

5

Time passed: _____

6

Time passed: _____

7

Time passed: _____

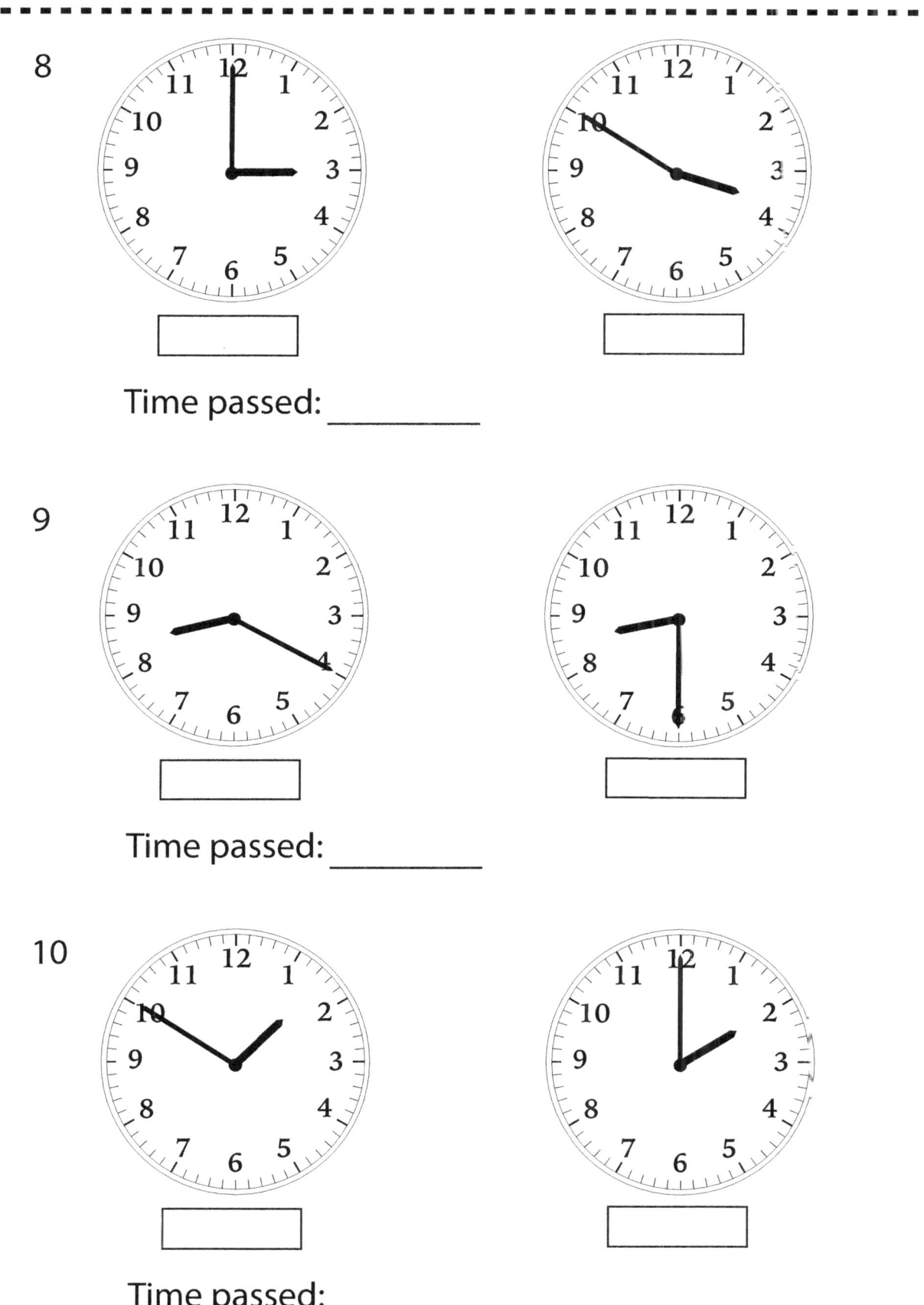

8

Time passed: _____

9

Time passed: _____

10

Time passed: _____

Word Problems telling time up to 5 minutes

1. Miranda starts reading at 5:45 and finishes at 6:20. How long was she reading for?

Answer: _____

2. Maya starts her spelling test at 10:00 and finishes at 10:25. How long did she work on her test?

Answer: _____

3. Louis starts his movie at 8:35 and stops it at 9:10. How long did he watch?

Answer: _____

Word Problems telling time up to 5 minutes

4. Ryan starts walking his dog at 2:35 and gets back at 3:05. How long did his walk last?

Answer:_____

5. Lucy starts playing a game at 7:30 and finishes at 8:20. How long did she play?

Answer:_____

6. Ben starts his chores at 10:20 and finishes them at 10:55. How long was he working?

Answer:_____

Word Problems telling time up to 5 minutes

7. Mirabelle takes a nap at 3:35 and sleeps for 40 minutes. Draw what time she woke up on the clock.

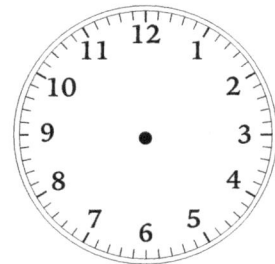

8. Payton wants to spend 30 minutes writing in her journal. She starts at 2:25. Draw in what time she should stop writing.

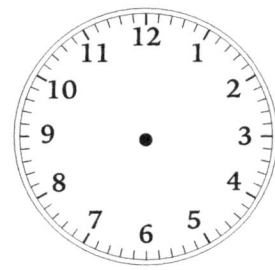

9. Ari spends 15 minutes every day cleaning his bedroom. He starts at 8:10. Draw in what time he should finish.

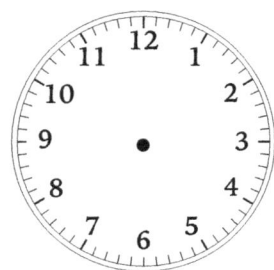

Word Problems telling time up to 5 minutes

10. Solomon swims in his pool for 45 minutes. He starts at 10:40. What time does he finish swimming? Draw it on the clock below.

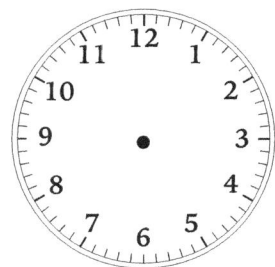

11. Peter starts cooking dinner at 5:55 and finishes 20 minutes later. What time does he finish? Draw it on the clock below.

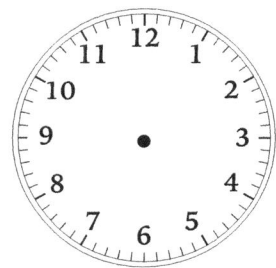

12. Michael spent 30 minutes at the park. He left at 10:15. What time did he arrive at the park? Draw in the time on the clock below.

Word Problems telling time up to 5 minutes

13. Molly wants to practice the piano for 40 minutes. She starts practicing at 5:30. What time should she stop practicing? Draw it on the clock below.

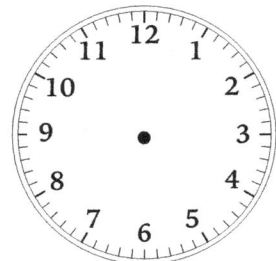

14. Roman was at his friend's house for 50 minutes. He left at 4:05. What time did he get there? Draw it on the clock below.

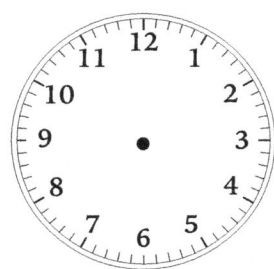

15. Rachel spent 25 minutes at the library. She left at 11:30. What time did she get there? Draw it on the clock below.

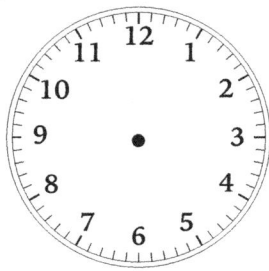

Word Problems telling time up to 5 minutes

16. Isabel spends 20 minutes at the store. She leaves the store at 12:35. What time did she get there? Draw it on the clock below.

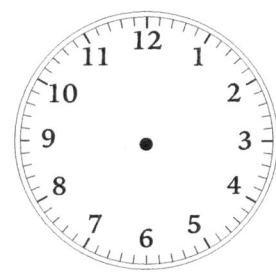

17. Olivia read her book for 55 minutes. She finished reading at 6:20. What time did she start reading? Draw it on the clock below.

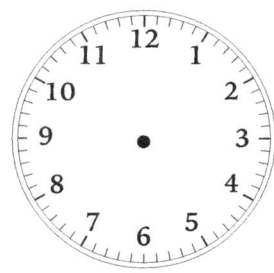

18. Jane spends 15 minutes working in her garden. She finishes working at 11:35. What time did she start working? Draw it on the clock below.

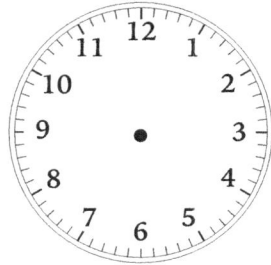

Telling Time up to the Minute

Every clock has 60 lines to help us tell time up to the minute.

This clock tells us that it is 3:30

This clock tells us that it is 3:31

This clock tells us that it is 3:32

This clock tells us that it is 3:33

Do you notice a pattern? We can use addition to tell time to the minute!

Fill in the blanks:

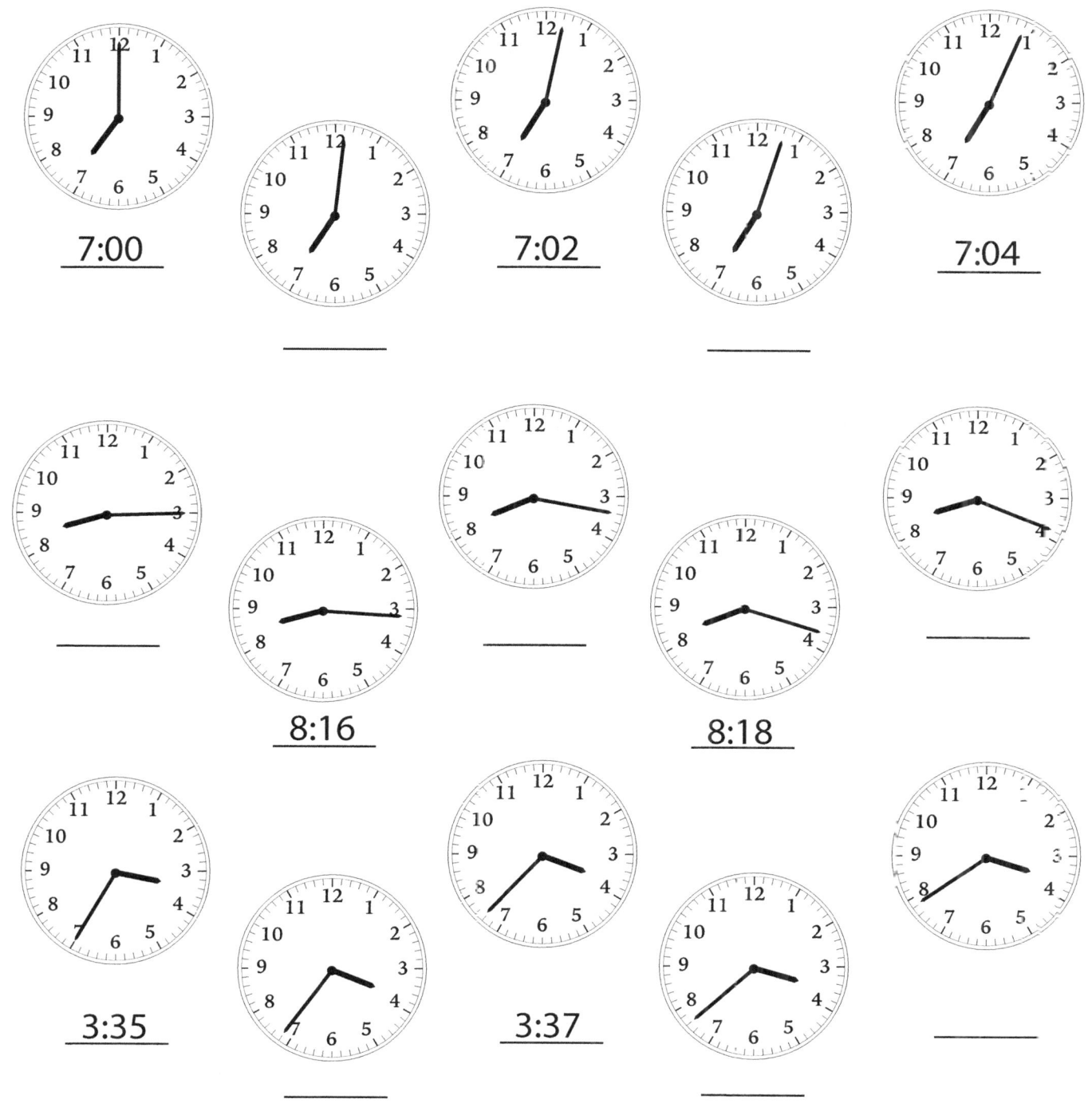

7:00

_____

7:02

_____

7:04

_____

8:16

_____

8:18

_____

3:35

_____

3:37

_____

Circle the Correct Time

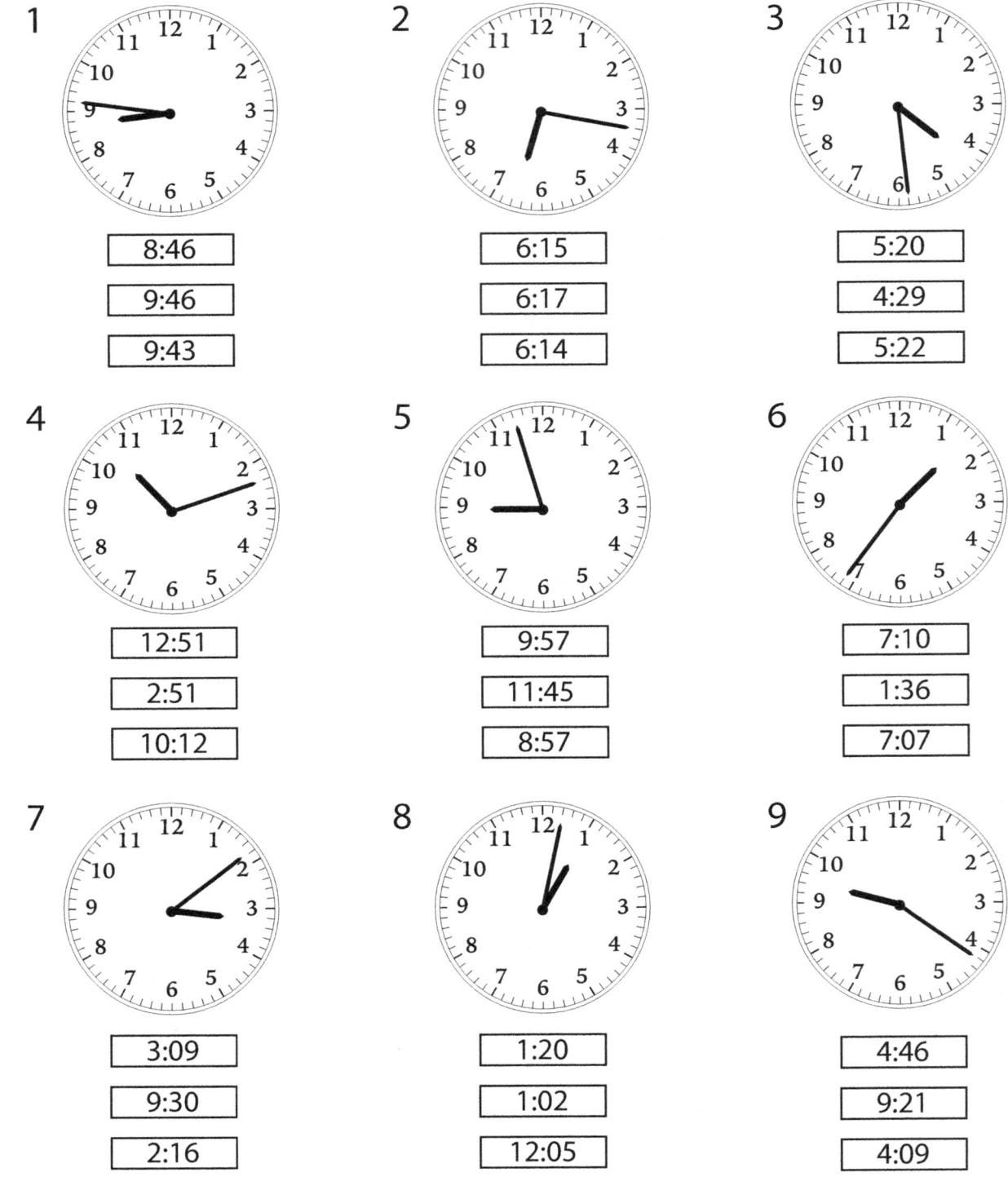

1

8:46

9:46

9:43

2

6:15

6:17

6:14

3

5:20

4:29

5:22

4

12:51

2:51

10:12

5

9:57

11:45

8:57

6

7:10

1:36

7:07

7

3:09

9:30

2:16

8

1:20

1:02

12:05

9

4:46

9:21

4:09

78

Circle the Correct Time

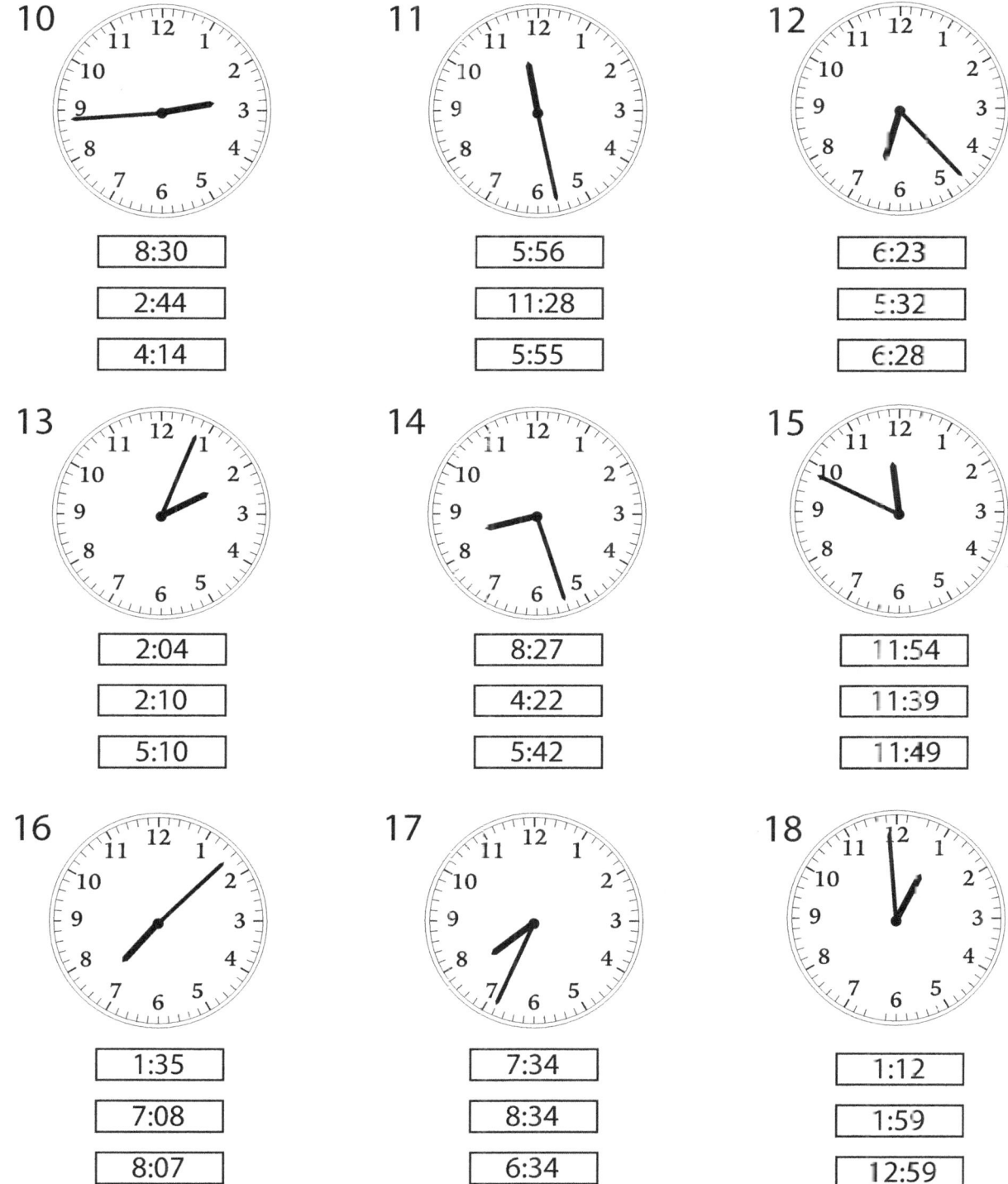

10
8:30
2:44
4:14

11
5:56
11:28
5:55

12
6:23
5:32
6:28

13
2:04
2:10
5:10

14
8:27
4:22
5:42

15
11:54
11:39
11:49

16
1:35
7:08
8:07

17
7:34
8:34
6:34

18
1:12
1:59
12:59

Circle the Correct Time

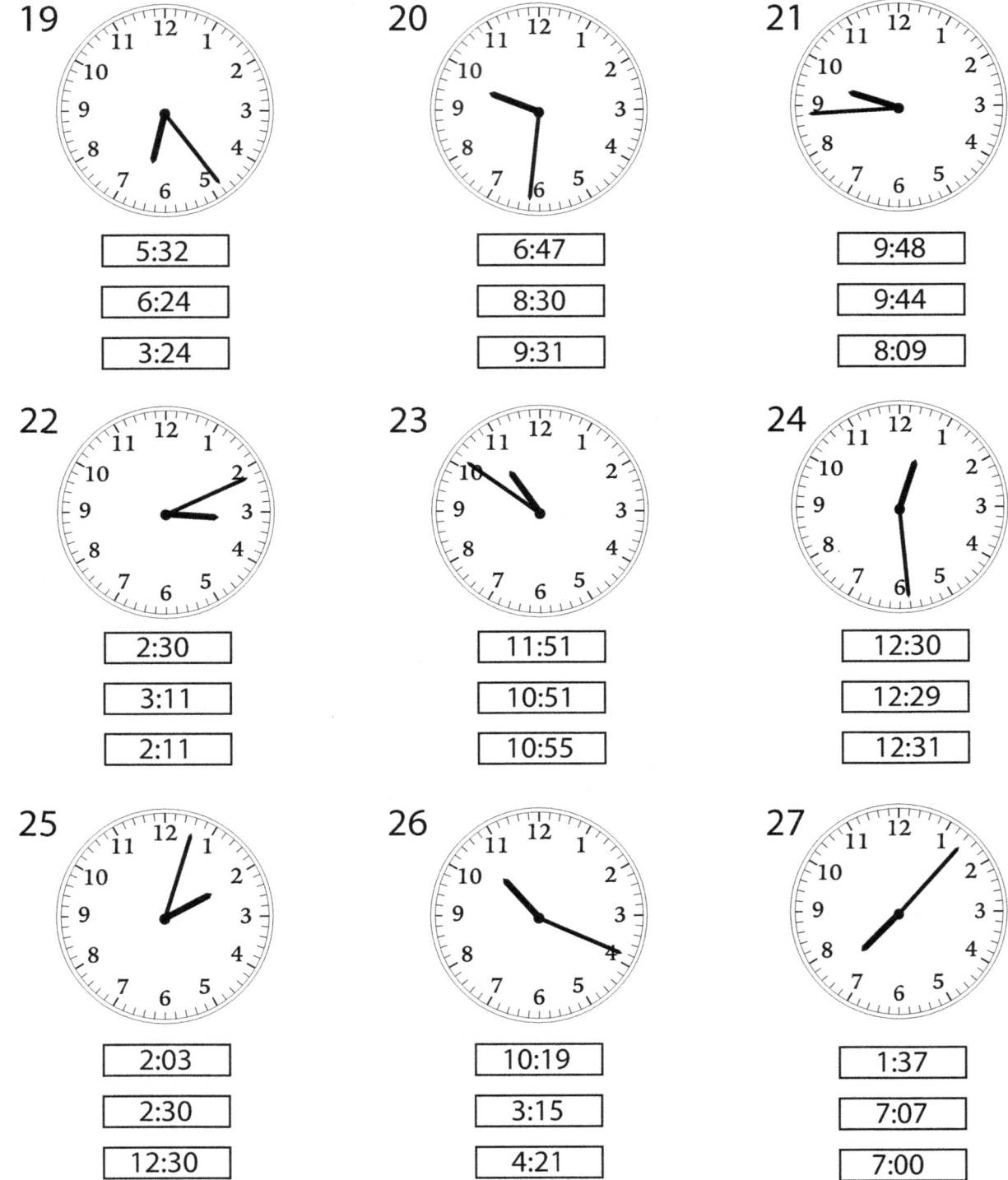

19

5:32

6:24

3:24

20

6:47

8:30

9:31

21

9:48

9:44

8:09

22

2:30

3:11

2:11

23

11:51

10:51

10:55

24

12:30

12:29

12:31

25

2:03

2:30

12:30

26

10:19

3:15

4:21

27

1:37

7:07

7:00

Draw a line to connect the clock with the correct time

1

5:13

2

9:33

3

8:57

4

11:02

Draw a line to connect the clock with the correct time

5

6

7

8

6:53

2:01

11:28

8:02

Draw a line to connect the clock with the correct time

9

10

11

12

9:05

5:04

6:38

3:46

Write in the Correct Time

1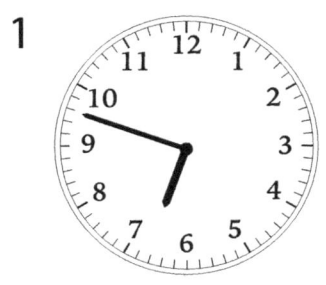

_____

2

_____

3

_____

4

_____

5

_____

6

_____

7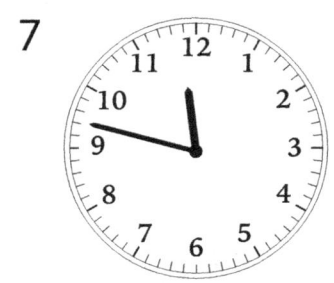

_____

8

_____

9

_____

Write in the Correct Time

10

_____

11

_____

12

_____

13

_____

14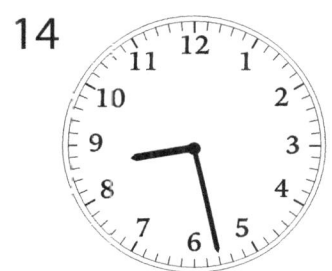

_____

15

_____

16

_____

17

_____

18

_____

Write in the Correct Time

19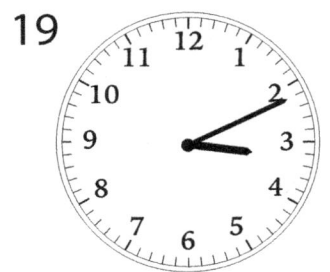

_____

20

_____

21

_____

22

_____

23

_____

24

_____

25

_____

26

_____

27

_____

Draw the hands on the clock

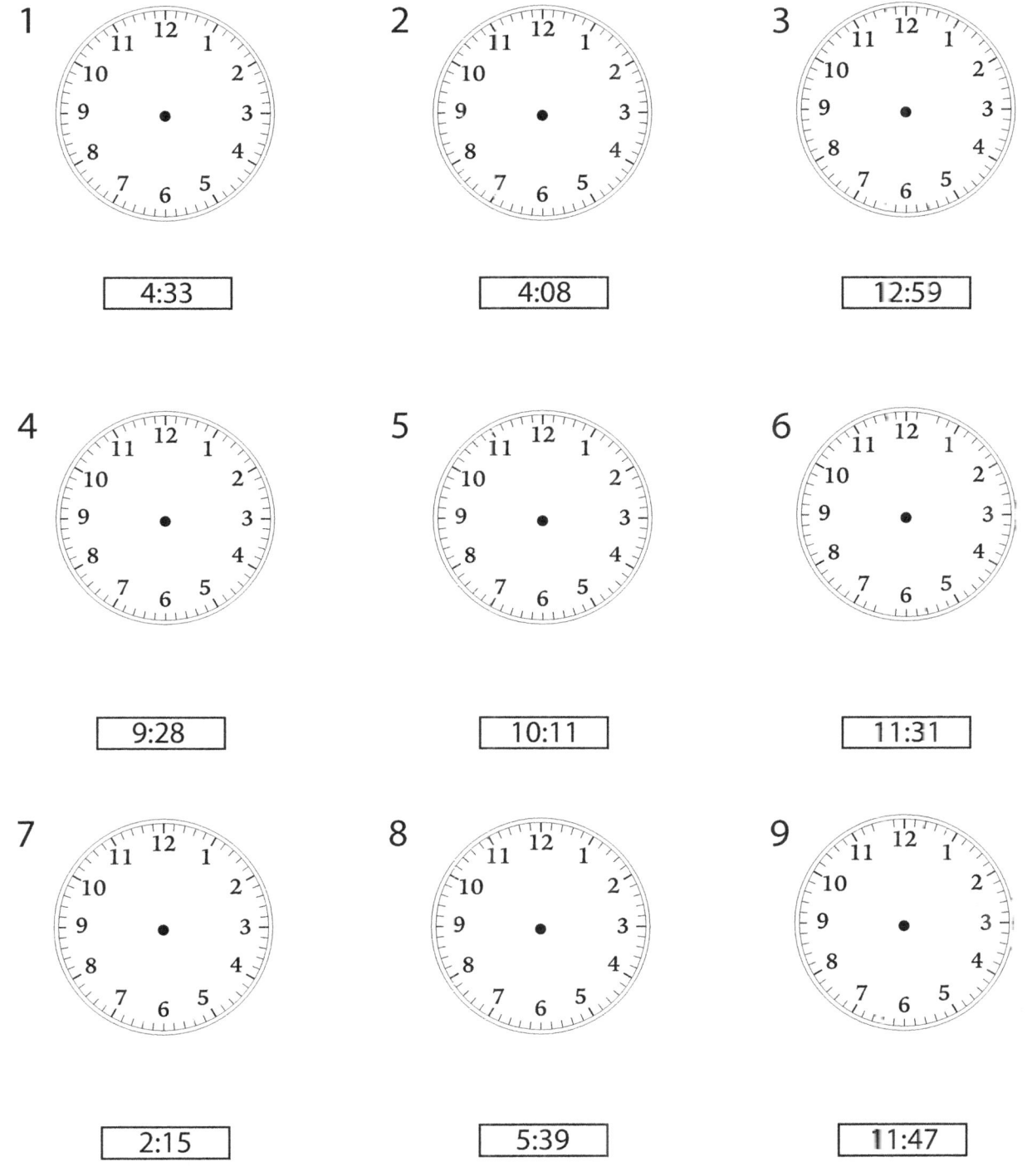

1   4:33

2   4:08

3   12:59

4   9:28

5   10:11

6   11:31

7   2:15

8   5:39

9   11:47

Draw the hands on the clock

10   9:12

11   7:31

12   11:13

13   1:37

14   8:21

15   12:02

16   9:09

17   6:36

18   8:56

Draw the hands on the clock

19   7:35

20   12:09

21   7:05

22   1:56

23   4:40

24   3:07

25   9:57

26   3:48

27   2:23

How much time has passed?

Look at the clocks and write in the time. How many minutes have passed?

Example:

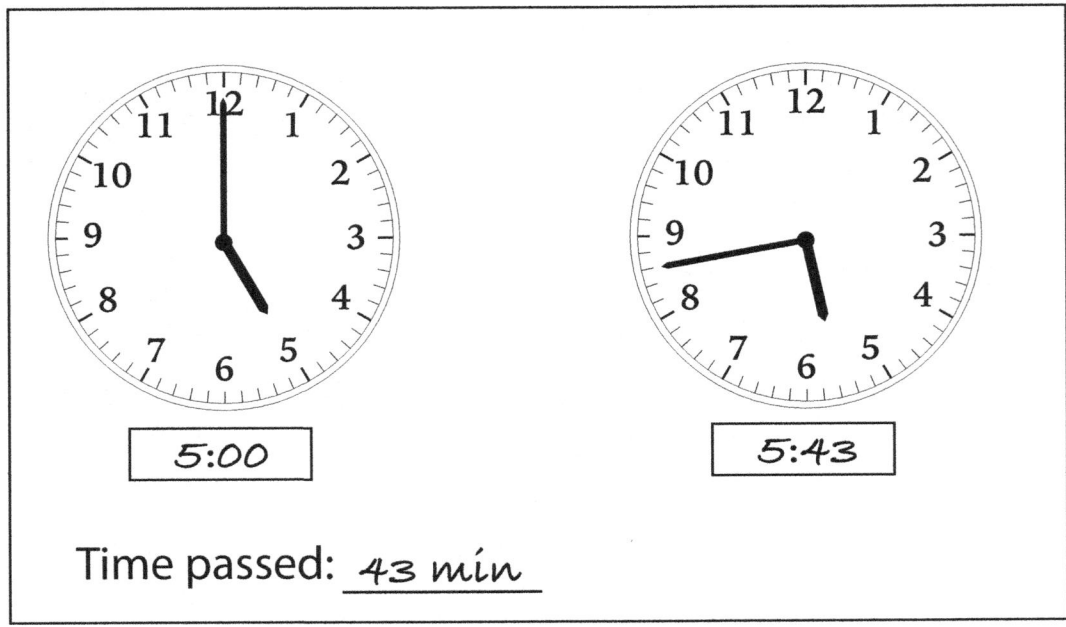

5:00

5:43

Time passed: 43 min

1

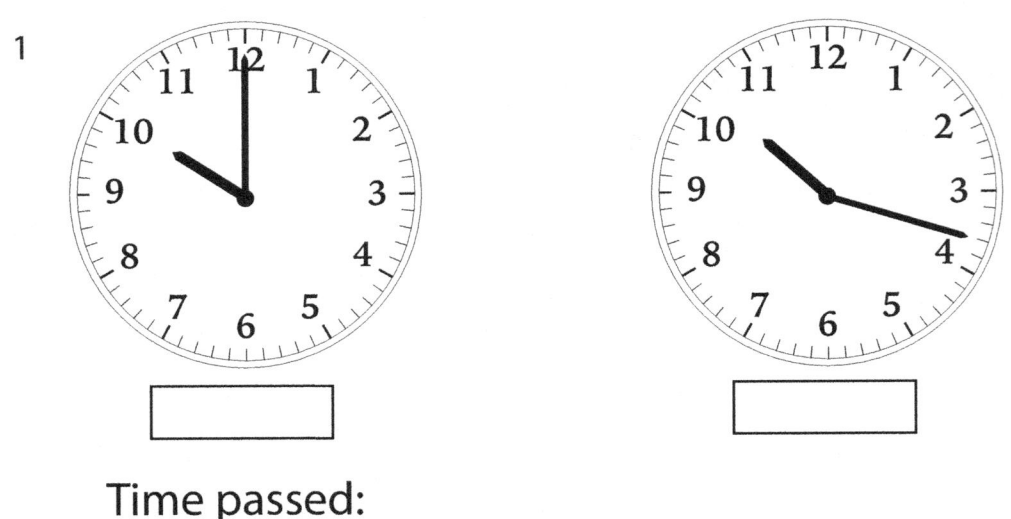

Time passed: _____

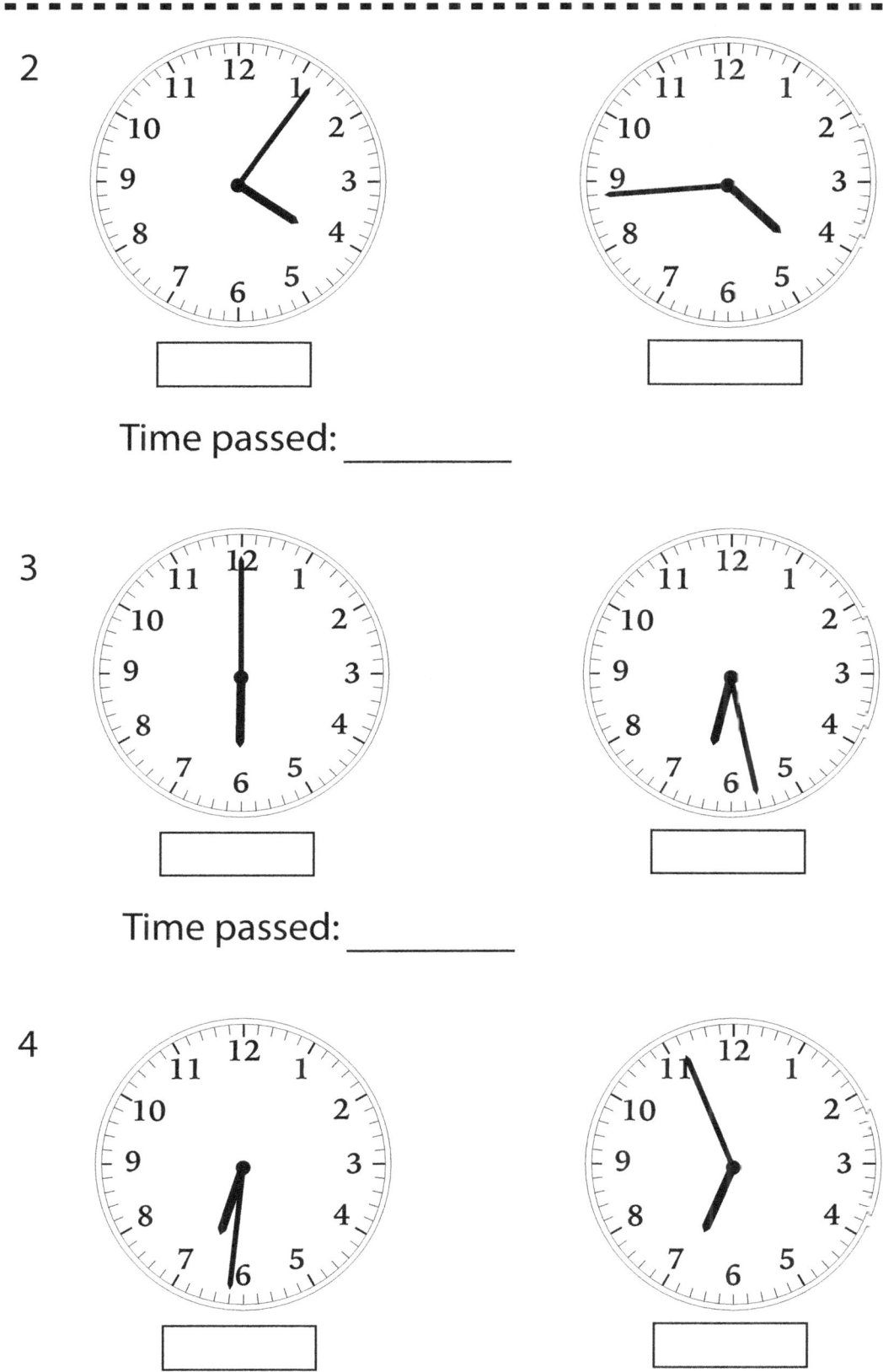

2

Time passed: _____

3

Time passed: _____

4

Time passed: _____

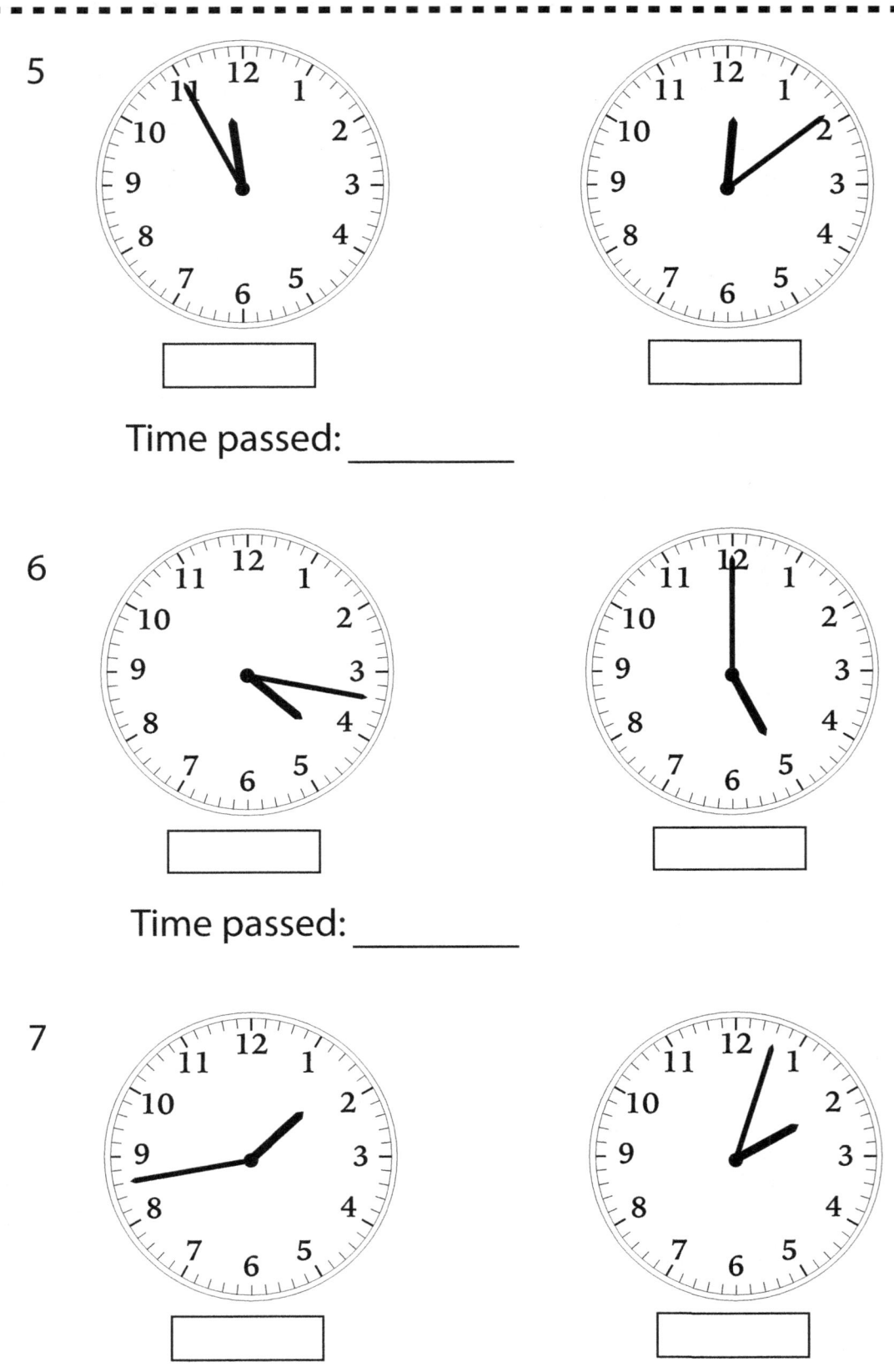

5
Time passed: _____

6
Time passed: _____

7
Time passed: _____

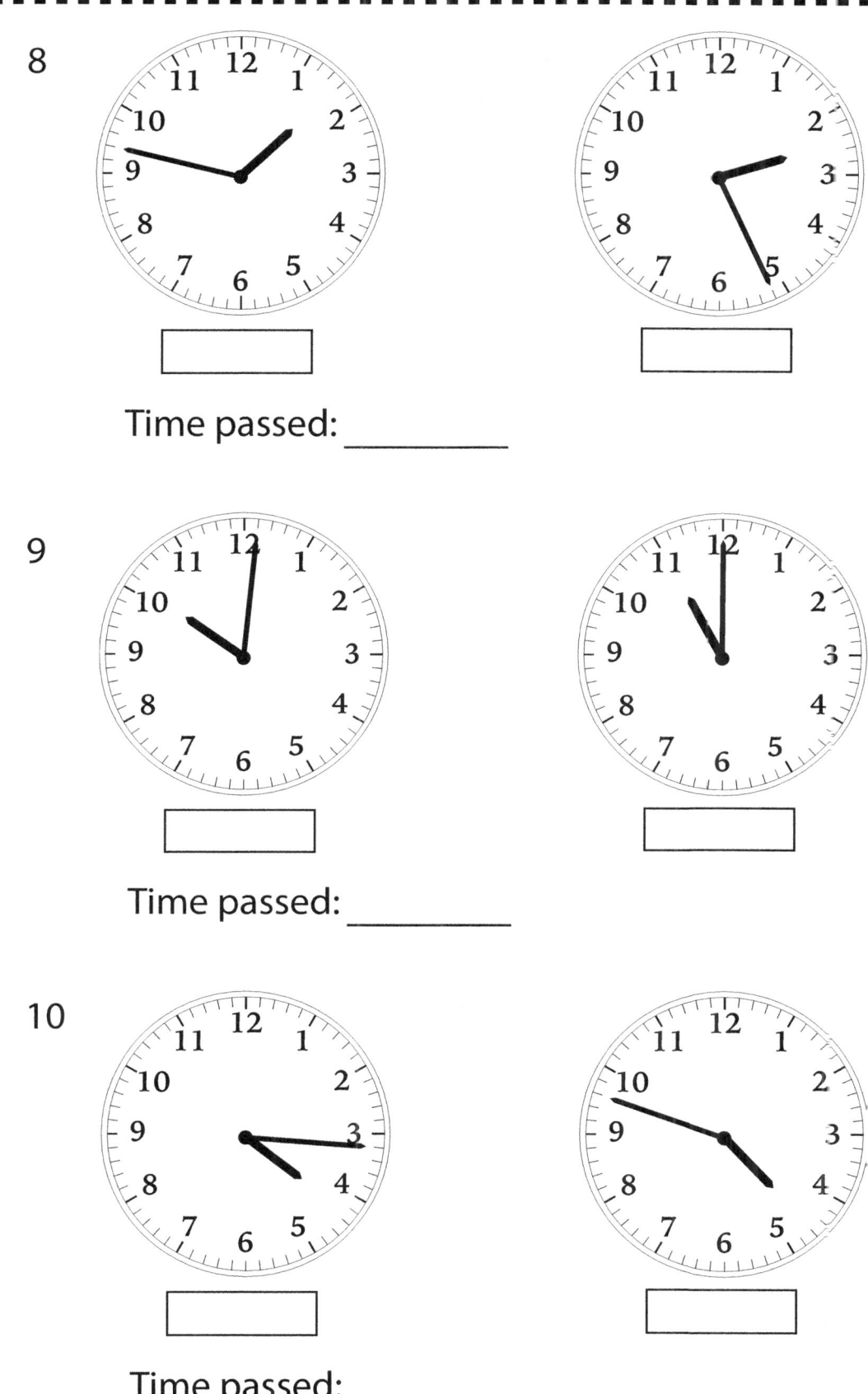

8

Time passed: _____

9

Time passed: _____

10

Time passed: _____

Word Problems telling time up to the minute

1. Katherine starts playing a video game at 6:34 and ends at 7:02. How much time did she play?

Answer: _____

2. Wendy starts driving to work at 8:04 and gets to work at 8:49. How long was she driving for?

Answer: _____

3. Marianne starts running at 1:00 and ends at 1:24. How many minutes did she run?

Answer: _____

94

Word Problems telling time up to 5 minutes

4. Eliza starts babysitting her brother at 6:45 and stops at 7:56. How many minutes did she baby sit?

Answer: _____

5. Noah starts his homework at 4:34 and finishes at 5:11. How long did his homework take him?

Answer: _____

6. Ben leaves for soccer practice at 6:29 and gets home at 8:43. How long did practice last?

Answer: _____

Word Problems telling time up to 5 minutes

7. Brianne left for the store at 5:10 and was gone for 43 minutes. What time did she get home? Draw it on the clock below.

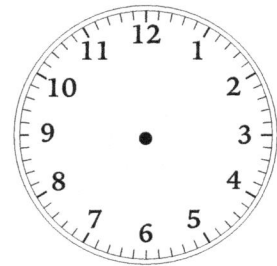

8. Lisa wants to spend 30 minutes working on her project. She starts working at 11:28. What time should she stop? Draw it on the clock below.

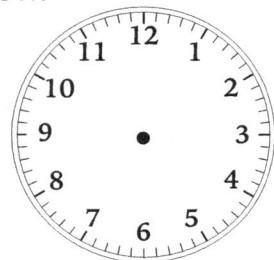

9. Bridget puts a cake in the oven for 30 minutes at 8:07. What time should she get the cake out? Draw it on the clock below.

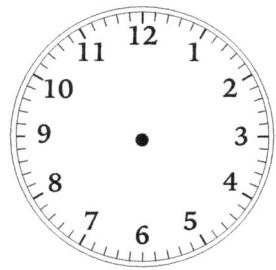

Word Problems telling time up to 5 minutes

10. Marta wants to practice her violin for 45 minutes. She starts practicing at 5:08. What time should she finish practicing? Draw in the answer on the clock.

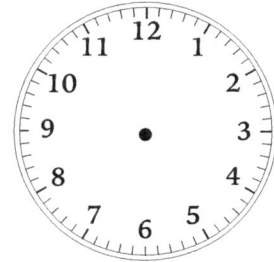

11. Avery plays basketball every day for an hour. Today she finished playing at 4:06. What time did she start playing? Draw the answer on the clock.

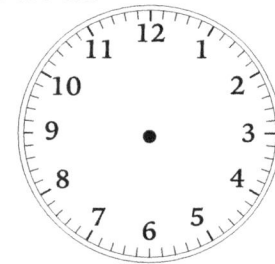

12. Lucas was at his friend's house for 35 minutes. He left his friend's house at 5:56. What time did he arrive? Draw the answer on the clock below.

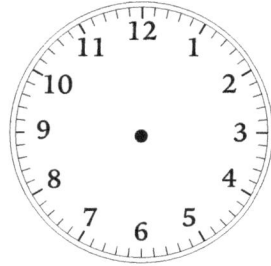

AM and PM

When writing the time we can use the abbreviations a.m and p.m.

a.m. stands for "ante meridiem" which means **before** noon
p.m. stands for "post meridiem" which means **after** noon

At 7:00 a.m. we wake up for school.

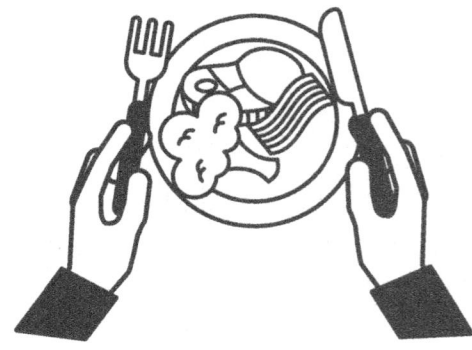

At 7:00 p.m. we eat dinner.

At 8:00 a.m. we take the bus to school

At 8:00 p.m. we go to sleep.

AM or PM?

Write in the time followed by a.m. or p.m. for each of the activities.

Eating breakfast

1 _____

Doing homework after school

2 _____

Taking a shower before bed

3 _____

Eating a snack after school

4 _____

Going on an evening walk

5 _____

Reading the morning paper

6 _____

Reading a book before bed

7 _____

Going to work early

8 _____

Going to a restaurant for dinner

9 _____

AM or PM?

Taking an afternoon nap

10 _____

Going to bed late

11 _____

Going on a morning jog

12 _____

Making dessert after dinner

13 _____

Watching the evening news

14 _____

The store opens at this time

15 _____

Playing during afternoon recess

16 _____

The sun rises at this time

17 _____

Going for a bike ride after lunch

18 _____

Answer Key

Page 5:
2. 4 o'clock
3. 9 o'clock
4. 2 o'clock

Page 6:
5. 6 o'clock
6. 1 o'clock
7. 8 o'clock
8. 5 o'clock

Page 7:
9. 11 o'clock
10. 12 o'clock
11. 9 o'clock
12. 10 o'clock

Page 8:
2. 3:00

Page 9:
3. 12:00
4. 7:00
5. 8:00
6. 10:00

Page 10:
7. 12:00
8. 6:00
9. 5:00
10. 9:00

Page 11:
11. 11:00
12. 4:00
13. 2:00
14. 8:00

Page 12:
1. 3:00
2. 11:00
3. 7:00
4. 6:00

Page 13:
5. 3:00
6. 5:00
7. 1:00
8. 12:00

Page 14:

1  2  3  4

Answer Key

Page 15:

5  6  7  8

Page 16:

9  10  11  12

Page 17:

13  14  15  16

Page 18:

1. 9 o'clock
2. 3:00
3. 2:00
4. 11 o'clock

5. 10 o'clock
6. 4:00

Page 19:

7. 7 o'clock
8. 1:00
9. 12:00
10. 6 o'clock

11. 8 o'clock
12. 5:00

Answer Key

Page 20:

1. 7:00, 10:00, 3 hours

Page 21:

2. 8:00, 12:00, 4 hours
3. 6:00, 9:00, 3 hours
4. 1:00, 3:00, 2 hours

Page 22:

5. 7:00, 11:00, 4 hours
6. 2:00, 9:00, 7 hours
7. 4:00, 8:00, 4 hours

Page 23:

1. 1 hour
2. 2 hours
3. 7 hours

Page 24:

4. 6 hours
5. 10 hours
6. 3 hours

Page 25:

7. 8 hours
8. 3 hours
9. 2 hours

Page 28:

1. 8:30
2. 8:00
3. 2:30
4. 1:30
5. 9:00
6. 11:00
7. 5:30
8. 1:20
9. 9:00

Page 29:

10. 6:00
11. 4:00
12. 2:00
13. 10:30
14. 7:00
15. 11:30
16. 2:30
17. 3:30
18. 1:00

Page 30:

19. 4:00
20. 7:00
21. 5:30
22. 1:30
23. 9:00
24. 12:20
25. 2:00
26. 4:30
27. 3:00

Page 31:

1. 4:00
2. 8:00
3. 2:30
4. 4:30
5. 9:30
6. 12:00
7. 3:30
8. 8:30
9. 7:00

Page 32:

10. 2:30
11. 7:30
12. 4:30
13. 8:00
14. 9:30
15. 10:30
16. 3:30
17. 2:30
18 11:00

Page 33:

19. 4:30
20. 8:00
21. 7:30
22. 11:30
23. 1:30
24. 2:00
25. 8:30
26. 1:00
27. 11:00

Answer Key

Page 34:

1
2
3
4
5

6
7
8
9

Page 35:

10
11
12
13
14

15
16
17
18

Page 36:

19
20
21
22
23

24
25
26
27

104

Answer Key

Page 38:
1. 6:00   6. 11:15
2. 4:15   7. 1:45
3. 2:45   8. 4:30
4. 5:30   9. 1:00
5. 8:00

Page 39:
10. 3:00   15. 5:15
11. 8:30   16. 6:45
12. 7:45   17. 2:30
13. 4:15   18. 7:00
14. 1:00

Page 40:
19. 3:15   24. 10:15
20. 8:30   25. 4:45
21. 11:45 26. 11:30
22. 8:15   27. 10:99
23. 5:15

Page 41:
1. 4:15   6. 12:45
2. 10:00   7. 3:15
3. 1:45   8. 4:30
4. 10:30   9. 1:00
5. 9:30

Page 42:
10. 3:45   15. 12:00
11. 5:00   16. 3:45
12. 1:15   17. 8:30
13. 10:30 18. 4:15
14. 9:30

Page 43:
19. 7:45   24. 6:00
20. 5:30   25. 3:30
21. 6:15   26. 2:15
22. 1:30   27. 7:15
23. 9:45

Answer Key

Page 44:

1 2 3 4 5

6 7 8 9

Page 45:

10 11 12 13 14

15 16 17 18

Page 46:

19 20 21 22 23

24 25 26 27

Answer Key

Page 47:
1. 7:00, 7:15, 15 min

Page 48:
2. 7:30, 8:00, 30 min
3. 4:00, 4:45, 45 min
4. 7:45, 8:30, 45 min

Page 49:
1. 45 minutes
2. 30 minutes
3. 30 minutes

Page 50:
4. 30 minutes
5. 45 minutes
6. 15 minutes

Page 53:
2. 11:50
3. 11:40
4. 11:25

Page 54:
1. 6:40   6. 3:55
2. 4:10   7. 12:45
3. 1:45   8. 8:25
4. 5:35   9. 10:05
5. 5:00

Page 55:
10. 4:40   15. 9:25
11. 3:05   16. 2:50
12. 7:45   17. 4:20
13. 12:20   18. 2:05
14. 1:00

Page 56:
19. 10:40   24. 11:45
20. 5:45   25. 5:25
21. 10:50   26. 2:35
22. 1:15   27. 10:00
23. 6:10

Page 57:
1. 1:15
2. 9:10
3. 6:30
4. 7:45

Page 58:
5. 12:55
6. 11:25
7. 4:40
8. 3:45

Page 59:
9. 12:55
10. 2:30
11. 9:15
12. 2:20

Answer Key

Page 60:

1. 4:10   6. 12:50
2. 6:35   7. 5:40
3. 4:30   8. 4:55
4. 1:05   9. 10:00
5. 10:15

Page 61:

10. 9:30   15. 12:40
11. 7:50   16. 4:10
12. 2:25   17. 2:30
13. 6:15   18. 7:00
14. 9:05

Page 62:

19. 5:45   24. 2:00
20. 9:55   25. 3:40
21. 1:30   26. 4:15
22. 12:05   27. 6:05
23. 5:10

Page 63:

Page 64:

Answer Key

Page 65:

19  20  21  22  23

24  25  26 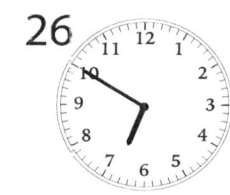 27

Page 66:

1. 10:00, 10:05, 5 min

Page 67:

2. 2:40, 2:55, 15 min
3. 6:00, 6:25, 25 min
4. 7:45, 8:00, 15 min

Page 68:

5. 5:05, 5:10, 5 min
6. 6:20, 6:35, 15 min
7. 11:30, 11:50, 20 min

Page 69:

8. 3:00, 3:50, 50 min
9. 8:20, 8:30, 10 min
10. 1:50, 2:00, 10 min

Page 70:

1. 35 min
2. 25 min
3. 35 min

Page 71:

4. 30 min
5. 50 min
6. 35 min

Page 72:

7  8  9

Answer Key

Page 73:

10

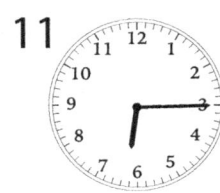
11

12

Page 74:

13

14

15

Page 75:

16

17

18

Page 78:

1. 8:46
2. 6:17
3. 4:29
4. 10:12
5. 8:57
6. 1:36
7. 3:09
8. 1:02
9. 9:21

Page 79:

10. 2:44
11. 11:28
12. 6:23
13. 2:04
14. 8:27
15. 11:49
16. 7:08
17. 7:34
18. 12:59

Page 80:

19. 6:24
20. 9:31
21. 9:44
22. 3:11
23. 10:51
24. 12:29
25. 2:03
26. 10:19
27. 7:07

Answer Key

Page 81:

1. 9:33
2. 11:02
3. 8:57
4. 5:13

Page 82:

5. 2:01
6. 11:28
7. 6:53
8. 8:02

Page 83:

9. 3:46
10. 9:05
11. 5:04
12. 6:38

Page 84:

1. 6:48
2. 9:03
3. 4:27
4. 1:05
5. 2:50
6. 1:21
7. 11:47
8. 8:03
9. 9:33

Page 85:

10. 9:30
11. 11:43
12. 9:58
13. 8:08
14. 8:28
15. 5:40
16. 2:14
17. 10:52
18. 10:00

Page 86:

19. 3:11
20. 6:36
21. 4:44
22. 5:24
23. 9:08
24. 2:01
25. 6:57
26. 4:15
27. 7:04

Page 87:

Answer Key

Page 88:

10
11
12
13
14

15
16
17
18

Page 89:

19
20
21
22
23

24
25
26
27

Page 90:

1. 10:00, 10:18, 18 min

Page 91:

2. 4:06, 2:44, 38 min
3. 6:00, 6:28, 28 min
4. 6:31, 6:56, 25 min

Page 92:

5. 11:55, 12:09, 14 min
6. 4:17, 5:00, 43 min
7. 1:43, 2:03, 20 min

Answer Key

Page 93:
8. 1:47, 2:26, 39 min
9. 10:01, 11:00, 59 min
10. 4:16, 4:48, 32 min

Page 94:
1. 28 min
2. 45 min
3. 24 min

Page 95:
4. 71 min or 1 hr and 11 min
5. 37 min
6. 2 hours and 14 min

Page 96:
7  8  9

Page 97:
10  11  12

Page 99:
1. 7:30 a.m.   6. 6:30 a.m.
2. 4:30 p.m.   7. 9:30 p.m.
3. 8:00 p.m.   8. 6:40 p.m.
4. 3:10 p.m.   9. 5:45
5. 7:15 p.m.

Page 100:
10. 2:20 p.m.   15. 9:15 a.m.
11. 11:50 p.m. 16. 1:30 p.m.
12. 6:00 a.m.   17. 5:52 a.m.
13. 7:25 p.m.   18. 1:00 p.m.
14. 6:15 p.m.

Made in the USA
Las Vegas, NV
13 June 2022